The

ENTREPRENEUR

Why 90% Fail the First Year and

How to Avoid the Mistakes They Made

Jim Britt

STAY IN TOUCH WITH JIM BRITT

www.JimBritt.com

www.CrackingTheRichCode.com

www.TheRichCodeClub.com

www.JimBrittCoaching.com

Email or to hire Jim as a speaker: support@JimBritt.com

THE RICH CODE CLUB

FREE members site.

www.TheRichCodeClub.com

The
ENTREPRENEUR
Why 90% Fail the First Year and
How to Avoid the Mistakes They Made

Jim Britt
All Rights Reserved
Copyright 2020
Cracking the Rich Code, LLC
10556 Combie Road, Suite 6205

Auburn, CA 95602

Jim Britt

The Entrepreneur

ISBN: 978-1-64153-339-3

DEDICATION

Entrepreneurs will change the world. They always have and they always will.

To the entrepreneurial spirit that lives within each of us.

God Bless America!

About Jim Britt

Jim Britt is an award-winning author of 13 best-selling books and numerous #1 International best-sellers. Some of his many titles include Rings of Truth, Do This. Get Rich-For Entrepreneurs, Unleashing Your Authentic Power, The Power of Letting Go, and Cracking the Rich Code.

He is an internationally recognized business and life strategist who is highly sought after as a success strategist and keynote speaker for all audiences.

Jim has served as a success strategist to over 300 corporations worldwide and was recently named as one of the world's top 50 speakers and top 20 success coaches. He was presented with the "Best of the Best" award out of the top 100 contributors of all time to the Direct Selling industry.

He has presented seminars throughout the world sharing his success strategies and life enhancing realizations with over 4,000 audiences, totaling over 1,500,000 people from all walks of life.

Early in his speaking career he was Business partners with the late Jim Rohn for eight years, where Tony Robbins worked under Jim's direction for his first few years in the speaking business.

As a performance strategist, Jim leverages his skills and experience as one of the leading experts in peak performance, entrepreneurship and personal empowerment to produce stellar results. He is pleased to work with small business entrepreneurs, and anyone seeking to remove the blocks that stop their success in any area of their life.

One of Jim's latest programs "Cracking the Rich Code" focuses on the subconscious programs influencing one's financial success, that keeps most living a life of mediocrity. His Cracking the Rich Code four-month program is designed to change one's money programming to that of the wealthy. More at www.JimBritt.com

What Other Professionals Say About Jim Britt

"Success is predictable if you know what determines it. Jim Britt offers valuable insights and strategies that will challenge you to leap beyond your current comfort level and stand up and be heard. If you want to strengthen your life, your mindset, your income and your effectiveness overall, Jim presents profound ideas in the most-simple, clear and easy to grasp manner. He offers practical wisdom for today's complex world."

Kevin Harrington, Star of the hit TV show Shark Tank

***

"Jim Britt's insights into the psychology of wealth will give you the focus, clarity and purpose to refine your financial plan and make the right choices for your business, your finances and your life."

Tony Robbins, NYT Best Selling Author, World's#1 Success Strategist, Motivational Speaker

***

"Jim Britt has been a friend and business associate for over 30 years. His work as a success coach, trainer and entrepreneur is remarkable. Work with Jim if you are interested in great success."

Jim Rohn, Best Selling Author, Top Inspirational Speaker

***

"I've known Jim since the mid 70's. He is a giant of a man and a giant thinker. If you ever get a chance to work with him do not hesitate. He delivers powerful, lasting, life-changing, results."

Mark Victor Hansen, Co-creator of Chicken Soup for the Soul

***

"They say that success leaves clues. After reading Jim Britt's book Rings of Truth you'll know what those clues are and how to use them. You'll want to keep it near you for quick reference, because you'll likely want to read it again and again on your way to success."

T. Harv Eker, NYT Best-selling Author, Secrets of the Millionaire Mind

"Jim Britt is an inspiring speaker and result-producing coach and mentor. He offers hope for a better future and the tools to make it happen."

Dr. Denis Waitley, Best Selling Author, Psychology of Winning

"Because of the work that Jim Britt does and the methods and techniques he uses to change your story and how you see yourself, it has enabled me to build my career and to make it against all odds."

Les Brown, World Renowned Motivational Speaker

Table of Content

Foreword by Kevin Harrington

Original Shark on the Hit TV Show Shark Tank

As Jim Britt says "Entrepreneurs will change the world. We always have and we always will." I totally agree. But if you are making the classic mistakes made by most beginning entrepreneurs, you will have a slim chance of being successful. Or, if you are already in business but find yourself working harder and harder just to make ends meet financially, then it could be that you are making one or more of the mistakes made by most in search of a better financial future.

The problem is that entrepreneurship is not taught in high school, college or on the job. Up until now only the lucky few either had a family member or close friend share these wealth building insights, or they simply stumbled upon them by sheer trial and error. Not a good way to plan your business or financial future.

I know Jim Britt. I know his work. I know the kind results he produces for those who attend his Cracking the Rich Code classes and read his books. What you have within this book is an amazing opportunity to tap into some proprietary wealth building strategies, that if applied could set you free financially.

For over four decades Jim has been empowering middle income individuals with a desire for more, to become successful, wealthy entrepreneurs. Not only are you going to receive some of the secrets of the wealthy, you'll know how to develop the mental toughness required to make it big financially in today's world. You'll also be inspired by some of the personal stories he shares.

Personally, I made all the mistakes in the beginning, but that all changed when I developed the mindset of the wealthy, which you will learn about in this book. I found that the most amazing thing about gaining wealth is how easy it is to attract once you know the rules of the game and play by those rules.

Can you just imagine the peace of mind you'll experience once you have your financial future handled forever? This book truly delivers!

Jim Britt doesn't pull any punches. He tells it like it is from personal experience as well as what he has learned from other professional entrepreneurs. You will get direct, action-oriented wealth building advice that works.

If you are not willing to act on the lessons and strategies in this content rich book, then my suggestion is you should not buy it. One the other hand I have found by hanging around with other wealthy people that the starting point for wealth is having a mentor and taking action. If you are one of those remarkable individuals who takes responsibility for your life and the results you produce, this book was written just for you and I urge you to hang onto every word. To be wealthy you have to seize opportunities as they arise. This book is such an opportunity. I know you were born to be wealthy. Act now!

Kevin Harrington

Original Shark on the Hit TV Show Shark Tank, inventor of the TV informercial and highly sought after speaker and success strategist www.kevinharrington.tv

Preface

*"The self-realized entrepreneur has a different concept about
failure and success. In fact, it is so different that neither exists."*

--- Jim Britt

We're all playing a high stakes game called life. You have only one
life in which to do everything you'll ever do. So, it's in your best
interest to step up, get focused, and find the fastest way to move on
your bucket list.

Ultimately, there are two options…you can spend the remainder of
your life accomplishing small stuff slowly…or you can learn to
upgrade your skill sets and mental programming regarding money
and success. There's nothing worth bragging about in getting rich
slowly, in learning a new skill set slowly, or in turning your business
around slowly.

Unfortunately, most of us have been conditioned to believe that
there is something wrong or illegal about achieving wealth quickly.
And, as someone who has repeatedly and consistently worked with
people and companies that accelerate from ground zero to major
accomplishments, "achieving success fast" is always my objective.
Transferring that reality to you is the purpose of this book.

I have a very simple philosophy when it comes to getting things
done. Once a decision is made, then every action you take is either
going to move toward your objective or further away. If you are
going to go all out to achieve a goal, might as well get it done in the
fastest way possible.

If this philosophy sounds appealing, you are in the right place. You
have to say goodbye to conventional ways of thinking, false
assumptions, old programming, mediocrity, and low expectations;
surrender the self-limiting and self-sabotaging beliefs you've clung
to regarding wealth and rapid success. They have no place in your
life unless you want to stay exactly where you are now. They only
serve to sabotage your performance, scare you into quitting, and put
you in the slow lane to success.

If you can't, won't, or simply refuse to accept what I'm about to share with you in this book, you will be making a huge mistake, one which will cost you in a big way. Quite frankly, if you desire wealth, you cannot afford to discount or frown upon anything in this book.

Think about it, if you want to become a wealthy entrepreneur, if you want to become debt free, why live with the pain of doing it slowly? Why not learn how to get rich fast?

Why should it take until next quarter or next year to become debt free? Today that changes forever, if you apply what I share in this book! Of course, most of us wish wealth and happiness to come more quickly. Since the beginning of time people have been trying to speed things up.

How do you accelerate your rate of success? How do you multiply your performance, exceed your highest aspirations, and achieve results on a scale that, in the past, seemed impossible? To start, stop thinking like the 90%. When you have someone who can help make things crystal clear for you, you can avoid mistakes, change your relationship with money, and shortcut success simply by listening to their advice–and then take action based on it.

When I first started out in business at age twenty-two, I had no idea how to accelerate my progress. In fact, I didn't even know where to begin. I had no coaches or mentors to teach or guide me. There were no examples for me to follow.

I relied, mostly on motivation, desperation, tenacity, and trial-and-error. This was extremely painful and slow. I had one person say to me, "Practice makes perfect." The reality was, I was practicing and perfecting the wrong thing. Lucky for me, after the first year of failing miserably, I met a man, a coach—a savior really—that shared with me the secrets to becoming a wealthy entrepreneur, fast.

It is my hope that my stories and strategies ahead will provide you with what you need to make good decisions, increase your profits dramatically, compress time, and put you on path to rapid financial results.

Over the years, I've learned to discipline myself by focusing only on the behaviors and strategies that gave me the biggest results in the shortest amount of time. And, if you want rapid rewards, you must learn to do the same. The great part about life is that you have a choice as to how you spend your time each day. So, doesn't it make perfect sense to concentrate your energy on the strategies that will give you the biggest breakthrough and results?

Time ruthlessly passes us by. It waits for no one. It is an unrecoverable asset, and unlike any other asset or resource, it cannot be reproduced, bought, sold, borrowed, stolen, saved, or modified in any way. All of us have the same 24 hours every day. When you spend an hour, you have one less to spend. All we can do is make use of it; that's the reason why we need to learn how to compress its use, to get more results faster, to shorten and reduce the length of time it takes to achieve your objectives.

Your thinking and behaviors act like powerful magnets pulling you and attracting the necessary people and resources you need for rapid results. The more focused your energies, the more passion you have, the more consistent your thinking and behavior, the faster you achieve results.

There are time gainers you must employ for rapid results: *decisiveness, discipline, consistent execution, laser focus, accountability, commitment to deadlines, 'do it now' attitude, tenacity, willingness to step out of your comfort zone.*

Just like a magnet can attract or repel, your behavior and thinking can work against one another if they are not in harmony. They can be two opposing forces moving in opposite directions and can lengthen or shorten the length of time it takes to achieve results. If not in harmony, they can aggressively work to expand and accelerate the distance between where you are and where you want to be. It's called a time drainer.

Let's look at other time drainers: *indecision, procrastination, excuses, blaming, inconsistency, fear, negative attitude, poor health, low self-esteem, and poor follow-through.* By engaging in any of these behaviors, you are sabotaging your chances of success, you are perpetuating pain, losing money, increasing tension, wasting time, compromising performance, and intensifying your own suffering by staying stuck where you are now. If you want to predict someone's chances of financial success, even your own, just watch how that person spends their time.

Bottom line: Time can only be used or wasted, and that's your choice. If you want to become wealthy, you need to learn how to use time to upgrade your execution skills, so that you can shorten the path and accelerate your rate of success.

Let's get started, shall we?

One

Overcoming Fear

*"Fear is taking a past experience, projecting it into the future with
the anticipation of it happening again, then re-experiencing it in
the moment."*

--- Jim Britt

Everyone has a fear that holds them back in some way. Everyone.
Otherwise, we would all be living the life of our dreams. Fear is the
friction in our thought process. Love or fear. Success or staying
stuck. That's a choice. The two emotions that we experience most
throughout our lives are love and fear. Understanding that fear is the
one thing that will move you away from what you'd love to have in
your life is a good place to start. Fear can be categorized as doubt,
worry, anger, anxiety, uncertainty, lack of clarity, and lack of self-
confidence. Fear is a made-up story about some event that has not
yet happened. It's a made-up story that will keep you stuck right
where you are, if you buy into it.

Let's do a little exercise:

Take some time and look at what you fear the most. Are you
doubtful about whether you can be wealthy? Doubt is fear based
and a made-up story.

Do you worry about money or success? Worry is fear based and a
made-up story.

Do you fear taking action? Are you holding back for some reason?
Both made-up stories. Take some time and decide just what it is that
holds you back and keeps you stuck where you are.

Ask yourself:

What am I afraid of?

How did this fear originate?

Who created this fear?

Is it real or a made-up story? (hint…it's made-up)

Do you like feeling the fear?

Do you want to let it go?

Are you willing to let it go?

When?

Most importantly, who would you be and what would you have without this fear?

What can you do right now that will move your financial world forward?

Your financial success will be determined by what you honor the most. Do you honor your financial success or your fears? No right or wrong here. It's just a choice to move forward or let fear run your life. Both are made-up stories! Both are a choice you make.

"I can't," or "the timing is not right," is what we say in order to keep pretending we aren't responsible for, or in control of where we are in life. Right now, take some actions that you may not have otherwise taken. Then, become aware of how that positive action influences your life.

Every change happens at the moment of decision. The fact is, indecision is a decision. It's a decision to be in the same spot next year. In other words, if you are struggling, a year from now you'll still be struggling if you don't make a decision and take action to change.

Remember this: every life level requires a different you. Every income level requires a different you. Every business level requires a different you. All require decision and taking action to change.

Remember: doing the same, produces the same. If that is working for you, by all means continue. If not…

FOR THINGS TO CHANGE, YOU HAVE TO MAKE A CHANGE.

Two

Just Quit Then

"The world contains incredible diversity, but you cannot experience it all within the confines of your comfort zone."

--- Jim Britt

John seemed embarrassed, his voice lowered, almost to a whisper as he spoke to me in a coaching session. He said, "Jim, I had so many goals going into this year. It's now the middle of April, and I'm so mad at myself. I haven't done anything."

I didn't say a word and there was a pause and a long silence on the telephone. It felt like forever. John then added, "I feel like just quitting."

I snapped back, "Sure John, go ahead. Just quit. Throw away everything you desire. How would that make you feel if you just quit? Better?"

"Not good," replied John.

I replied back firmly, "So cut the crap, John. We're in the 4th month of the year. The year

isn't close to being over. You even have 10+ days left in April. You could look

backwards or look forwards. Which way do you want to look?"

"Forward," said John.

I then asked, "What are two things you want to accomplish in the next 30

days, John? Write them down." John wrote them down and read them back to me. I then asked, "When will you be accountable for the 1st goal being done? And the 2nd goal? What actions do you need to take to get going NOW?"

John kept writing, then hesitantly said, "My procrastination and lack of focus have haunted me all year. In fact, all my life. I'm scared it's going to get the best of me."

I interrupted and jumped in, "Stop being scared and start doing something about the problem. Take action damnit! Action is the antidote for procrastination and fear. In fact, it is the only cure. You are allowing lack of focus to rip cash right out of your hands." I started to get a little stronger because I wanted him to get it. "Listen, you have 10+ days left this month. You can make excuses, or you can generate excitement in your life and in your business. You have to make the choice now. Are you ready to go out there and kick some butt?"

John came back with an enthusiastic, "Yes! Yes! I will do it!"

I said, "Let's do it then! Let's get going! I'll help you and guide you, but you have to do the work!"

John said quickly and with excitement in his voice, "I gotta go, Jim, I have calls to make, people to see, and money to earn!"

I overheard another conversation at a Starbucks the other day—a negative conversation. From gas prices and the economy to layoffs, this person was complaining about everything. This person defeated himself. The economy didn't defeat him. His boss didn't defeat him. He defeated himself.

That's the power of your own suggestion. It can cause you to win or it can defeat you. This is very important. It's so easy to look to the left or look to the right and find somebody complaining about something. And it's often easier to join in. Misery loves company, or so they say. I wouldn't know. Well, do not do it. Do not engage. You were not born to complain. You, my friend, were born to WIN. I know it. You know it!

Make your own economy. Work on yourself. Become valuable to others. Become attractive to others. Become a problem solver for others. Pass on the spirit of a hero, a winner!

Today! Start speaking triumph over your life!

Do you realize how many people in the world are complaining about how bad things are right now? That talk never ends. Do not engage.

Do you realize how many people are wasting their time on unproductive actions right now?

Do you realize how many people have given up on their dreams in life?

Do you realize how many people are satisfied with mediocrity and have no interest in improving their life?

=Take a deep breath=

Right now, you've opened this book, and you've committed your time and energy to improve yourself just by reading it.

Do you really realize how unique you are that you're committed to improving and being your best?

Do you really realize that your commitment to a better life will soon inspire your family, friends, strangers, and future generations to be inspired?

Do you really realize how important you will be to somebody, somewhere, very soon? Maybe the very next person you meet.

Stop waiting for a certain event or condition to happen to become great. Be great today! Tomorrow will happen tomorrow. Focus on right now and today. Focus on what will bring you results today!

Realize how successful you are—feel it deep down inside, enough to want to be your best.

Don't let anyone or anything bring you down. You're above that—way above! The world is waiting to experience your gifts, talents, and abilities.

I'M HONORED THAT YOU'RE READING THIS BOOK RIGHT NOW. I AM. I REALLY APPRECIATE YOU. LET'S GET STARTED!

Three

The Most Powerful Word

"Progress is impossible if you continue to do things the way you've always done them."

--- Jim Britt

I can't prove this, but my guess is this is the most popular word in the world, and the second most powerful. But, before I share it with you, let me say this. If I decoded the successes I've had, I can trace them all back to a powerful word, not the most popular. Simple, but powerful. Now, the easiest, and I bet most "popular," word spoken in the world is, "No." This is the popular word of the 90%. Most people use this word too much. Way too much! It is like most people's best friend. I used to use this word a lot, but then something happened and everything changed.

From my #1 best-selling books, to the success of my businesses, it all traces back to the most "powerful" word. But, hang on. I'm not the only one who's tapped into it. Tony Robbins, Jim Rohn, Richard Branson, Brendon Burchard and many, many others, in all sorts of businesses, have as well.

Here it is:

Your greatness starts by saying "YES" to an opportunity. 90% of the world is inclined to say "No" before they even consider a good opportunity, and that's the reason they remain in the 90% lower income earners.

I remember saying to my first mentor, "I can't afford it."

He said, "Stop right there!" He said, "Your mind just shut down, plus your focus is 'can't afford,' which means you'll create more of the same." He said, "There is always a way, you just have to figure out how."

Then I said, "The timing just isn't right."

He said again, "Hold on Jim. Stop right there." He said, "I want you to remove that statement from your vocabulary." He said, "The timing is never right for great opportunities. You'll never hear a highly successful person say, 'The timing isn't right,' or 'I don't have the time.'" He said, "If you want something bad enough, you make the time."

Right now, there's an opportunity for you to do something great. Will you say ,"Yes?" If there were opportunities to get around more action-oriented individuals, Would you take action?

Imagine yourself being great now—becoming that Key Person of Influence in your field of business. Close your eyes and see yourself winning big! How does that feel? Why not be your best self. Take action. Say, "YES!" Then figure out how.

One simple word has changed the world so many times. "Yes." I want you to consider this as you begin your preparations from this point forward.

We're facing some difficult times, and at the same time, we're entering a new world that is filled with hope, filled with people saying, "YES" like never before!

What will you say, "YES" to this year?

Will you say yes to more money?

A better business?

Changing the lives of more people?

A new home?

The best vacation of your life?

All too often I find that people are more willing to say, "No" than they are to say, "Yes." We may say, "Yes" but our mind chatter is saying, "No." We all come up with fabulous reasons (excuses really) why something didn't happen—none of which are really valid in the end.

One year ago, what did you want to say, "Yes" to, but never followed through on? Was it your health, weight, or exercise? How about your income level? I've found that there are only a finite number of things that in the end keep us from getting to our "Yeses" each year, and they're usually the same things, year after year.

As much as you really, really want to attract more business, help more people, make more money, etc., about half-way through the year most realize that it's not going to happen. I've done it. It's just human nature to say, "No" and make up some excuse, simply because it's easier than saying, "Yes."

I remember in my first business, my goal for the month was $10,000. At the beginning of the month, I would tell everyone, "I am going to earn $10,000 this month." Around the middle of the month, I would make up some excuse and lower my goal to $5,000. Then around the 25th of the month, I hadn't earned a dime, so I would disappear until the new month started with a new goal of $10,000 for the month. I had a whole list of excuses. It was a rainy month. It was winter and no one was out and about. It's the holiday season? (when did we add that season anyway?)

I want to encourage you to say, "YES" for the next twelve months, non-stop! **YES!** Just one word, but a powerful one! This could change everything for you. But if you say, "YES" get ready to put on your running shoes. We're going for a success ride and our destination is your brightest future.

Are you in or definitely IN?

Ready?

Are your shoes laced up?

Hold on~

Let's go!

WHAT WILL YOU SAY "YES" TO IN THE NEXT TWELVE MONTHS?

Four

What is Your Purpose?

"If you do what you do with love, you'll have only what you love in your life."

--- Jim Britt

If you've ever struggled with finding your purpose in life, your reason for being here on planet Earth, then listen up, because you do have a purpose.

The reality is, every person ever born and everything ever created, has a definite purpose. Every insect, animal, tree, blade of grass, every human, everything has a purpose.

There is a specific reason as to why you exist too, and it should be your life's responsibility to find it and share it with the world.

Consider all the components of your body. Your brain's purpose is to allow you to think, reason, and make choices. Your heart's purpose is to pump blood that delivers oxygen so the rest of your body can live. The purpose of your lungs is to make breathing possible. Your feet, your eyes, your nose, your fingers, your ears, your vocal cords, every aspect of your body has a purpose. So, if all of the components of your body were created for a definite purpose, don't you, the overseer of all those things, have a purpose too?

So, the question is, what is your purpose? What is the reason you exist? What big impression are you here to make on the world? What legacy will you leave? You will only be truly happy when you follow your purpose; so make it your purpose to discover your purpose.

When I was a child, I used to pretend to be a superhero. What it would be like if I could accomplish anything I wanted in life? Superman was my favorite hero. In fact, at age eight, to see if I could fly, I tied a large towel around my neck and jumped off a 14-foot high barn roof. Luckily, I landed on my feet. Please don't try this at home.

And for some reason, I don't know why or when, we stop believing in the things we did as a child. We all seem to lose touch with what we believed then, with our ability to imagine great things. Maybe it's social pressures, peer pressure, and later in life, professional pressures that seems to bury the imagination and passion we once had. We are taught maybe by well-meaning parents and teachers to get a job, get paid, experience a yearly pay raise, then retire in 40 years and be happy.

I dropped out of high school in the 10th grade. Years later as I entered the speaking business with the late Jim Rohn, I was told by hundreds of people that I should write a book about my life story. I would reply, "I'm not good at writing," or "English was my worst subject, and I don't think anybody would read what I write." But after writing my first book, Rings of Truth, with the help of a talented person, I discovered that I could in fact write, and have a passion for it. To date I have written 13 books, this one is #14—and more to come.

Right now, there is something that you have always thought about doing. You think about it, yet you don't do it. Why? You have your reasons, no doubt. And you repeat these reasons to yourself over and over again, just like I did for years about writing. I can tell you that self-talk you repeat to yourself, or you tell others, is not valid and you are missing out big time.

If your reasons are something like, "I can't start a business because earning money in my current job is more important," or "I don't know how to run a business. Besides, I don't have the money to start a business," maybe you are afraid of what others would think if you failed. Excuses. ALL excuses.

Making money is about solving problems, and there are plenty of problems to choose from in the world today. Find a problem you care about and start working to solve it. Maybe you are not going to fix a certain problem by yourself, but you can contribute and make a difference. And that feeling of making a difference is ultimately what's most important for your fulfillment and purpose.

The enemy to passion and purpose is most always complacency and procrastination. We get into our routines. You know, "By the time I get home it's late. I have time to mix myself a drink, have dinner, and watch a little TV. I don't have time for anything else." We distract and lie to ourselves. The couch is comfortable. The popcorn is tasty, but there's no time left for passion and purpose.

This is a problem. Passion and purpose are created as a result of trying on a few things to see what fits. It can become a trial and error process. You may not know how you feel about a certain activity until you engage in it.

I remember in my 20's I tried bowling as a recreation. I wasn't very good at it at first. In fact, I sucked at it. Then, I hired a pro to teach me. The more I practiced the correct way, the better I got at it and the more passion I developed for the game. six, 300 hundred perfect score games later and an average league score of 226, I developed a passion for it. It also became a money-maker for me on the side.

My youngest son, Walker, graduated college with a 4.0 average and a degree in Marketing and Business. His passion, however, was in the gaming industry, playing video games online. In the game Halo, he and his brother, Warren, were ranked #1 & 2 in the world. This led Walker to playing another game where he has fans that pay to watch him, play with him, and be coached by him. He now makes a great living doing what he is passionate about, playing video games.

We try to find that one thing that we are meant to do; but, trying to find only one thing is the reason why we sometimes feel like something is missing. The notion that we have only one thing we are meant to do, I believe, limits us from fulfilling our true greatness. Take me for example; I have multiple things I do. I'm a life coach, business coach, entrepreneur, author, speaker, and mentor. These are my passions. When you get in touch with your passions and lead a passionate life, you are living your life on purpose. You fall in love with what you do and can't imagine ever doing anything else.

Let go of the idea that there is only one purpose for you. Stop resisting the unknown and fully engage in what is happening right here, right now. When you live a passion-filled life, you are living on purpose; and that is the purpose of life. That feeling that something is missing goes away when you lead a passion-filled life, and with that, you discover your purpose.

WHEN YOU LIVE A PASSION-FILLED LIFE, YOU ARE LIVING ON PURPOSE, AND THAT IS THE PURPOSE OF LIFE.

Five

Taking a Giant Leap Forward

"All beliefs are false until you decide they are true, then only true for you."

--- Jim Britt

Finally... the "Ah-Ha!" moment!

I have made a ton of mistakes in my life—many of them several times. Being a rational person, when I came up against something that wasn't working out the way I wanted, I approached it like having a flat tire on my car. I fixed the tire and continued down the road. Makes sense, right?

But what I discovered was, I kept driving down the same road with the same potholes and nails. My "flat tires" always felt familiar.

See, you... I... everyone... have these "programmed" beliefs and habit patterns that keep us going down the same road, changing or replacing the same tires, and generally repeating the same mistakes. All the self-help, "think good thoughts" and "think really hard and attract it" programs we've tried don't work in the long run because they're just short-term patchwork solutions, like fixing the tire.

Finally, the "Ah-Ha!" moment! It was like a spark of understanding, an awareness that was "given" to me as a gift, simply for asking the questions I was asking. I figured a few things out. Call them "secrets" if you will, but I'm not about to take ownership. It is information we all have available to us. We are just too busy changing flat tires to see them.

I realized that instead of trying to get the things I wanted by working harder, learning more, or getting motivated, I would get far better results if I could <u>let go</u> of the things that were keeping me from getting what I wanted. Trying to get ahead without letting go of your old beliefs and habits patterns is like trying to get up a mountain while carrying an elephant. It's just not going to happen, and you're likely to get squashed!

That one simple shift in thinking changed my focus, took me in a brand-new direction, and ultimately had a major effect on my long-term success and happiness.

Moving forward means that you have to go beyond your comfort zone of what's familiar, beyond the current you. Every income level requires a different you. And a different you, requires letting go of the old you. Taking that giant leap forward does not mean gambling or risking everything you have. It simply means that you take advantage of opportunity instead of ignoring it. It means that you let go of the excuses you have always used to avoid taking action. You simply frame the opportunity and take a 360-degree view, looking at it from different angles and then taking appropriate action if it looks right for you. For example, if an opportunity required money and you had no money, look at the opportunity as if you had money instead of just saying to yourself, "I have no money." Then, if the opportunity looks real and profitable, ask yourself, "How could I raise the money?" There is always more than one way to get the job done.

Being willing to take a risk and take a full 360-degree view will unmask the truth, revealing the only thing that may be standing in your way. And once you know the truth of the situation you can choose whether to take action or not.

If you want wealth, you must risk believing in yourself and the decisions you make. You have to make the assumption that you *can* become financially successful at whatever level you choose. Otherwise you risk settling for only a small fraction of what life could provide for you. I'm not talking about taking a big chance, but rather giving yourself a chance.

The solution is not to challenge the odds of success, but rather to challenge your limiting beliefs. Until you challenge the limiting beliefs of what you think you can achieve, you'll never know how far you can go. Remember, a belief is something that you have decided is true; but the reality is that it may not be true at all.

The idea here is to learn to suspend your beliefs and look for the real truth. Instead of deciding whether something will or will not work, look for evidence proving beyond any doubt that it can or cannot work. And if you decide it can work, act as if success is absolutely guaranteed.

You may have some trouble believing that you can move forward quickly, so look at it this way: it is said that a human being only utilizes about 10% of his or her brain. What that means to me is that humans are in a resourceful, productive state only 10% of the time. The rest of the time they are lost in non-productive belief systems, caught up in circumstances and old negative habit patterns that no longer serve their greater good, or trying to control things that are beyond their control. Let me ask you this. What if you could double your effectiveness to 20%? What would that do for your productivity and earning power? What if you could be more productive just 20% of the time? How about 30% or 50%? What would happen if you applied that to earning more money?

My point is that everyone has the potential to do much more than what they are currently doing! It may be that you are skeptical because you've never done more than 10% before. I get it. You only have the factual data about yourself, based on past history and programming. Doubting yourself that way is called "mind chatter," and it will ruin your chances at success if you let it.

If you buy into the mind chatter, your thinking will always be flawed and so will your productivity. At some point in their lives, most people simply accept "flawed thinking" as "correct thinking." The question is, how do you know if your thinking is flawed or if it is correct, based on truth? You challenge it! Who taught you to think and believe that way? What if they didn't know the truth? What if the person who taught them didn't know? How did it really work for them? Was the person, or persons, who taught you about money wealthy? What did they know about creating wealth?

As a child you took bold steps and big risks; you challenged yourself to learn to sit, crawl, and walk. Later, you challenged yourself to ride a bicycle, swim, etc. You had faith that you could do it, didn't you? Now is the time to dig deep inside and challenge yourself, rediscover that faith. It's time to put those inhibiting beliefs to rest and go for it with everything you've got.

Again, for now, just suspend your beliefs. I don't want you to believe me. All I want you to do is give it a go and see what happens. You don't even have to be convinced that you will succeed in a big way. All I ask is that you don't keep hanging onto limiting beliefs about your personal limits. Just hold off on believing anything for now. Remember, you do have a choice.

Just start to act as if you have complete faith that you will become wealthy. What that means is to merely do what you would do if you knew you were going to become wealthy. Have complete confidence and conviction.

Doubt is the biggest problem and does the most damage. Doubt creates uncertainty. Uncertainty creates lack of clarity. And lack of clarity immobilizes. So, don't give doubt any mental space. Move forward boldly as if it was absolutely incomprehensible that you would experience anything other than success.

To achieve more in less time, you have to create some inner chaos for yourself. That's the only way you know you're truly making progress that will last. So be prepared for the possibility of confusion, anxiety, and failings along the way. That's just part of opening yourself up to new strategies that have the potential to deliver maximum performance gains.

Just remember, when stepping out into something new like starting a business, problems are part of the process. In fact, problems are the reason you are going into business! They are not proof that your ambitions are futile or that you should give up. Businesses solve problems. That's the nature of business. Look at it this way: problems create opportunities. And taking advantage of the opportunity by solving the problem is how people get rich. The bigger the problem you solve, the more potential for earnings.

Creating wealth is all about the choices you make. Very often, however, we say we have no choice; in reality, what we really have is a very difficult choice. You've no doubt heard yourself say things like, "I have no choice. I have to work 70 hours a week," or "I have no choice. I can't make the meeting."

In such situations, "I have no choice," really means, "The choice is too difficult to make, so I'll pretend it doesn't exist." This type of thinking can be a trap. You can pile up one "no choice" on top of another until your life seems completely out of control.

No matter where you are or what you are doing, you do have a choice about almost everything you do. You have chosen the path to where you are right now, and you have complete control over where you are going from here. You may have chosen to become financially independent, and you have complete control over whether it becomes a reality or not. You can choose success, or you can choose to let your circumstances dictate how you live your life. It's a choice.

Yes, some choices will indeed be difficult, but there's nothing to be gained by denying them. The next time you catch yourself saying that you have no choice, stop and ask yourself, "Is this really true? Is there another choice I could make that would serve me better?"

The way to improve your business, your finances, your circumstances, and your life is to make the choices that will take you to where you desire to be. Have the courage to look at those choices and carefully consider their implications. Ask yourself, "What will the outcome be if I make this choice? Is there a choice I could make that would better serve me?" Decide to take complete control of your financial success, and your life, and make the choices that will move you in the direction you want to go.

YOUR LIFE AND YOUR FINANCIAL STATUS CAN BE DIFFERENT AT ANY TIME YOU CHOOSE TO MAKE DIFFERENT CHOICES."

Six

Money Programming

"Don't let your experiences from the past dictate how you live your life in the present. The past is simply a memory, it doesn't exist in real life."

--- Jim Britt

All of us have programs embedded in our subconscious that will determine our financial status.

Have you ever wondered why some people seem to get rich easily, while others are destined for a life of financial struggle? Is the difference found in their education, intelligence, work habits, skills, luck, timing, contacts, or maybe their choice of businesses or investments?

The answer is none of the above!

No doubt you've read other books, listened to audios, videos, attended seminars, and learned about various money-making systems, whether in real estate, stocks or business online. But what happened? For most people, not much! They get a short blast of motivation, and then it's back to the status quo.

There is a simple answer though, it's a law, and there is no way around it. It all comes down to this: if your subconscious "money programming" is not set for financial success, nothing you learn or know and nothing you do will make much of a difference. Yes, if you are going to become a salesperson, for example, there are certain selling skill sets you need to learn. However, you can learn them all and have the very best sales techniques, but if your money programs are not set for wealth, you will never become wealthy. I'll explain more about this later.

Like many of you, I had an obsession with earning more money. I thought I had a lot of potential but had little to show for it. I read all the books, listened to all the audios, and attended seminars. In fact, one of my first seminars was a Dale Carnegie sales course. I graduated top in my class. I really wanted to be successful. I don't know whether it was the money, the freedom, the sense of achievement or just to prove I was good enough, but I was obsessed with becoming a success financially. Unfortunately, nothing seemed to be working.

My first business, I did exactly as I was told. I worked hard for a year but was not making any money. I thought that I was fairly intelligent and a good person, and I couldn't understand why the one thing that I wanted, financial success, completely eluded me.

Then, I got some advice from a wealthy man. He said, "Jim, if you want to be successful at business, you need to do what successful business people do." He said, "Rich people think differently. If you want to be rich, start thinking the way rich people think and start doing what rich people do."

Using some of the principles he taught me, I became a millionaire in one year. And today, my mission is to share with you the same principles he shared with me, and more.

In this book, I'll be sharing how each of us is conditioned to think and act about money, and what you can do to change it. You'll discover why some people are destined to be rich and why others are destined for a life of struggle. You'll understand the root causes of success, mediocrity, or financial failure, and how to begin changing your programming so that it works for you instead of against you.

The big question is, "What is your subconscious programming regarding money?"

We've all heard stories of those that have accomplished great things financially. My friend, the late Bill Bartmann, was once the 23 richest persons in America, worth an estimated $6 billion.

Then, he lost it all due to some major mistakes his partner made. So, here is this multi-billionaire who had lost everything. You would think that he might be looking for a bridge to jump off, but not Bill. He started rebuilding, and within a few years, he was on track to having it all back again, in the same industry no less. Why? His money programming is set for "high." On the other side of the coin, we have lottery winners. They win millions of dollars and within five years virtually half of them are back where they started. Why? Their money programming is set for "low."

This is how your money programs got created. We are all taught how and conditioned to deal with money. Unfortunately, many of us, like myself, were taught by people who didn't have a lot of money. Their way of thinking about money became our natural and automatic way to think.

Your mind is nothing more than a big and spacious hard drive. In your hard drive you file and store information. It's your programming about every aspect of your life. Where does this programming come from? It comes from your upbringing, your life experiences, and the experiences and programming of those around you. Parents, grandparents, peers, friends, the media, TV programs, your own experiences, etc., all have a hand in your programming.

So, how are you conditioned? You are conditioned in three primary ways in every area of life, including money.

The first is verbal programming. What did you hear when you were young? Did you ever hear phrases like:

- Money is the root of all evil.
- Save your money for a rainy day.
- Rich people are greedy.
- Rich people are criminals.
- You have to work hard to make money.

In my household, every time I asked my father for any money, he'd get a pained look on his face no matter the amount, because he knew there wasn't enough to go around. It wasn't that he didn't want to give it; it was that he couldn't afford it and still support the family. His money programming was set for "low."

Every statement you heard about money when you were young remains lodged in the subconscious programming that is running your financial life today. Naturally, you don't even have to think about it. You don't even see it. When you engage in any new money-making activity, you search your money file and decide what you're going to do. Your subconscious programming determines your core belief when it comes to earning more money. Your core belief determines your decisions, and your decisions determine your actions, which eventually determine your outcomes.

The second is modeling. What did you observe when you were young? I'm sure you've heard the saying, "Monkey see, monkey do." Human beings are not far behind. Generally, we are a combination of both of our parents in the arena of money, as well as other things in life.

So the question is, what were your parents like around money when you were growing up? Was money always a struggle in your home or was it a source of joy and ease? Whatever your answers, your life will be very similar, if you don't change the programming.

On the other side of the coin, some of us are exactly the opposite of one or both parents when it comes to money. Many people who come from poor families are determined to become wealthy. Whether such people get rich or work very hard trying to become successful, they usually aren't happy. Why? Because they often use anger as a source of motivation to keep them moving forward and making more money. The more money they have or strive for, the angrier they get.

The reason or motivation you have for making money, or creating success, is vital. If your motivation for acquiring money or success comes from a non-supportive root such as fear, anger, or the need to prove yourself, your money will never bring you happiness.

The third is specific incidents. What was your experience about money? The primary way we are conditioned is by specific incidents. What did you experience when you were young about money? These experiences are extremely important because they shape your core beliefs, or rather, the illusions you now live by regarding money.

If you had a painful experience with money——like the pain of being embarrassed because you couldn't do what the other kids in high school were able to do—it's no wonder, then, that as an adult you subconsciously want to spend all you have in an effort to get rid of the pain of the past.

Now it's time to answer the big question. What is your current money programming set for, and what results is it producing for you? Are you set for mediocrity and financial failure or set for wealth? Are you programmed for struggle or for ease around making money?

As I stated earlier, your money programming will determine your financial status, which can have an effect of all areas of your life. If you're a woman whose money programming is set for low, chances are you'll attract a man who is also set for low so you can stay in your financial comfort zone and validate your programming. If you're a man who is set for low, chances are you'll attract a woman who is a spender and gets rid of all your money, so you can stay in your financial comfort zone and validate your programming. As humans, we will go to almost any extreme to prove to ourselves and the outside world what we believe is true, even to our determent.

So again, how can you tell what your money programming is set for? One of the most obvious ways is to look at the results you have produced thus far. Look at your bank account, cash flow, net worth investments, and business success.

In the same way, the only way to change your level of financial success permanently is to reset your money programming. If you want to change the visible, you must first change the invisible. What's in your subconscious programming is what has produced the results you are currently experiencing. So, focusing your attention on what you have already produced will do you no good at all. You can't change the outcome you have already produced. You can, however, change to outcome for days and years to come. But to do so, you have to change your subconscious programming regarding money.

THE ONLY WAY TO CHANGE YOUR LEVEL OF FINANCIAL SUCCESS PERMANENTLY IS TO RESET YOUR MONEY PROGRAMMING.

Seven

Overcoming Self-Imposed Money Limitations

"Progress is impossible if you continue to do things the way you've always done them."

--- Jim Britt

One of my favorite analogies—that most of us, at one time or another, can identify with making money, or the lack of—is about the determined fly.

You've no doubt witnessed a fly beating its head against a window trying desperately to get to freedom. It's a life-or-death futile attempt to fly through the glass. You can tell by the sound that in its mind it's thinking, "I must try harder. But it's just not working!" Or maybe a fly can't think, but you get the picture.

No matter how hard it tries, we both know that the fly will never break through the glass and is doomed to die. We also know, with just a few seconds of flying in the right direction, it could be free from its self-imposed trap, with only a fraction of the effort. Yet it continues to beat its head against the glass until it dies. Without a doubt, this approach makes sense to the fly; otherwise it would stop!

This is how most people feel when it comes to making more money. No matter how hard they try, they end up year after year with a repeat performance of the last, and in the end with barely enough to survive. While it does require some effort, the point is that trying harder is not always the solution to earning more. They say that, "Practice makes perfect," but that's not altogether true if you are trying harder, persisting, and practicing the wrong thing, like the fly.

Let's face it. Most of us from time to time feel that life is just one big financial struggle with a series of never-ending money problems. Yet the truth is that life does not have to be that way. In fact, it can be just the opposite. Earning more should not be about struggle. Earning more is about pursuing and creating what you truly desire in an easy, stress-free manner. Think about it. Which is easier, struggle to earn more, or have all you want?

Let me ask you a serious question. Do you really want to earn more, but it seems to elude you? And why is it that it seems like such a struggle to create the things we want anyway? Here's the real answer: if you are not earning all the money you want, it is because your subconscious holds some contradictory intentions. In other words, you want something and your subconscious tells you that you are not capable based on past experiences.

For example, you might say, "I want to earn more money," but your dominant subconscious programming may be, "Earning the amount of money I want seems impossible," or "My past experience says I have tried many times and failed." Notice anything different about these statements? Of course! One program wants more and the other says it's impossible. That's what creates the struggle. You are going in different directions. It's like driving your car with one foot on the accelerator and the other on the brake and wondering why you are not getting anywhere.

So, what is this "subconscious mind" that seems so mysterious? The conscious mind is simply the one you are using to read this book or to make decisions about your life affairs. The subconscious mind is your programming, the sum total of all your experiences in life. It is designed to protect you from repeating past mistakes by offering you feedback on a decision you are about to make. You touched a flame as a child, and you got burned. Now, when you get near a flame, your subconscious brings up the past experience, and you know not to touch the flame. This all happens as an automatic subconscious response that is never even registered in your conscious mind.

The reality is, because of past programming, past experiences, your conscious and subconscious are almost always in conflict. You <u>consciously</u> say, "I want more money," and then after listening, your <u>subconscious</u> checks in and says, "Hold on a minute. Money was hard to get for your parents," or "Remember when you lost everything before, so you don't need to try again," or whatever. So, you conclude, based on past programming, that no matter what you do, it is too difficult to create that amount of money." As a result, there is no agreement between the conscious and subconscious to make a change, so they cancel each other out. Therefore, you give up on creating more money.

What's important to understand is that the two different agendas are creating a feeling that actually attracts that which you do not desire instead of what you do desire.

Let me explain to you what is really happening.

Once a firm decision is made to have more money (doesn't matter how much) the message is sent to the subconscious. It is then carried out with precision, unless an old program is brought forth offering conflicting information. This is where you have to become consciously aware of the input from your subconscious (mind chatter). You make a decision and immediately start having doubts. You have to stop and let go of the doubt, so that your subconscious continues to act upon the decision you made rather than the doubt.

Look at it this way. You Google "making money" and up pops 4,250,000,000 results in 0.76 seconds. Which ones do you look at? The first page and maybe the second. Does that make them the best? No, they get on the top of the search by traffic.

So, when you say, "making money," your subconscious acts like Google. It brings up the top 10 about your experience with making money, in a split second, without your conscious mind having time to think it through. You say I am going to make a million dollars this year. Your subconscious says, "Hold on now! Here's the result you produced the last ten times." And if you don't become consciously aware of this happening, your conscious and subconscious are already in conflict.

It's called The Law of Cause and Effect, which we will discuss in more detail. It is always working. You just have to become aware that it is working to your advantage or disadvantage.

Once a decision is made, one that doesn't allow for anything less, and that message is sent to your subconscious as fact, what you have firmly decided begins its journey back to you. It is no longer susceptible to any argument whatsoever. The subconscious mind cannot argue. It only acts. It accepts the conclusions of the conscious mind as final. So, the point is, that you have to consciously override what the subconscious is telling you, just like pushing "delete" on your computer.

To put it simply, every decision you make has its own energetic vibrational harmony. That decision is impressed onto your subconscious mind. Then, through the Law of Cause and Effect, it will energetically bring into your view people, opportunities, situations, etc. that have a vibrational harmony that matches and supports yours.

So, when you receive what you don't want, it simply means that your conscious decision has been overridden by a conflicting program. Why? Because the decision was not one that sent a firm signal to the subconscious. If you send a half-baked decision, ("I am going to give becoming wealthy a try and see if it works"), what are you sending your subconscious to create? What vibrational harmony are you creating? When you look at what you are currently receiving, you'll know exactly what you are sending.

Your subconscious mind cooperates completely with your conscious decision when it *understands* and *agrees* with what you consciously want. In other words, when the decision is firm, your conscious and subconscious are not in conflict.

So, what do you do to change? Begin to consciously observe when you are feeling any emotional conflict. That is your inner guidance, your intuition, telling you that you are not acting in harmony with your decision.

Once the decision is made, the next step to change is the act of self-observation. When you feel conflict, act as though you have come to an intersection with a red light flashing and a sign that reads: Right turn on red after stop. Then, ask yourself before you proceed, "Is this action going to take me in the direction I want to go, or am I acting on old programming?"

If you do nothing else, remember that you MUST correct and STOP the negative influence IN THE MOMENT IT HAPPENS if you are serious about getting rid of self-imposed limitations and becoming wealthy.

So, how would you rate your performance to date? Are you achieving the results you want with the effort you are expending? It's impossible to change if you don't do something in a different way. The problem is that we most often go with the obvious. We rely on the same thinking, same habits, and behaviors we've used in the past, productive or not, because it's what we know. In fact, most of us are like the fly on the window, trying harder and harder, doing more of the same and getting nowhere fast. We resist new approaches because they make us feel more at risk, more uncomfortable. Know this, financial success is just outside your comfort zone. If you are not uncomfortable, you are most likely not making progress.

Make sure that you have a burning desire, backed by a firm decision and an internal heat hot enough to move past just wishful thinking. Let your vision and decision for a better future consume you and drive your actions. Only your vision, decisions, and passion hold the power to allow you to go the distance. Let your (mind) decision and vision direct your actions, and let your heart (passion) take charge of your move forward!

Decide what you are worth and then feed the feelings that fuel your passion by letting go of what disempowers you. Give yourself permission to go after what you want most. Give yourself permission to earn more. Let your deepest desires to be wealthy, direct you. Set your sites high enough so that you challenge yourself to live fully. Otherwise a part of you remains asleep, your talents remain hidden, your income remains the same, and your performance becomes that of a constant state of struggle.

Many of us can be found flying too close to the ground. Too often we don't give ourselves permission to soar! Stand up for yourself the next time someone tells you that you can't achieve something or when your subconscious offers all the reasons that you could fail.

It's time to start focusing on possibilities, rather than on limits and obstacles. All limitations are self-imposed, and all beliefs are limiting. If you want to doubt something, doubt your limits. Start to act as if your success is guaranteed, and then see which set of ideas you should believe in.

All limitations are self-imposed, and you have to learn to let go of them if you want to make progress. You don't have to settle for things as they are now. Your circumstances can change dramatically when *you* make a firm decision to change.

As human beings we most often go with the obvious. We fall into the trap of relying on old behaviors to attain new heights. This approach simply cannot and will not work. Your most dependable behaviors can become major obstacles that can and will cripple your progress.

When you change, life will give you a breakthrough experience. When you let go of the you that got you where you are today, a new you will appear. You'll then be able to jump to a higher orbit of achievement, live your dream, and enjoy a completely different level of success.

Here's some action items to consider as you make progress through this book.

1. Decide what you want to accomplish and make a list. Then, realistically look at what's holding you back from attaining each item on that list. Once you have decided what you want to accomplish and what's stopping you, you can move forward.

2. Now, this is critical…realize that every action you take from this point forward is moving you closer to or further away from accomplishing what you want. The question is, which do you honor most, your *objective* or your *obstacle*?

3. When you encounter any obstacle—doubt, worry, fear, subconscious programs, or even other people's opinions— stop like an alarm clock went off. Then, look at your choices and only take action that will lead you toward your objective. Evaluate your progress daily and you'll be amazed by the results.

Now, as you proceed through this book, you're going to have to shift gears a bit from what you are used to. You're going to be asked to develop and follow new patterns of thought and action. Because the rules of what works and what doesn't always change when you are attempting to make a move from normal performance to peak performance. Just remember that more of the same produces more of the same, and for things to change in your life, you have to make changes. So be bold and get ruthless about trying something different.

LET'S MAKE TODAY JUST 1%, OR MORE, BETTER THAN YESTERDAY. YOU IN? AWESOME!

Eight

Cause and Effect

"Everything in your life becomes different when you become different."

--Jim Britt

Cause and Effect is universal because it does not matter who you are, where you live, what your religious beliefs are, or what year you were born. It is true for everyone equally. It is as true as the Law of Gravity. Drop a coin and it falls to the ground. How often? Every time!

However, most often we use it by default rather than deliberate choice. We just go through our day focusing on problems that need to be solved or on things that don't feel good. In so doing, we are actually creating more problems and more of what does not feel good.

Think of yourself as a huge magnet. The kind that pulls metal to itself from far away. It doesn't try to pull the metal to it, it simply does it by its nature. The same holds true for you. Whether or not you are trying to create, you ARE doing so all the time. And you create what you focus upon. If you are focused on lack, you are creating more lack. If you are focused on something you love, you are creating more of what you love. I know it sounds incredibly simple, and it is.

We humans are actually very powerful creators, and we can use this wonderful, God-given power to create more of what we want in life, simply by paying attention to where we focus our attention.

An old saying goes, "As a man thinks in his heart, so is he." It's interesting that the writer of this said, "thinks in his heart," because most of the time we think with our mind. However, it is from the heart that we create. The heart is the transmitter of all signals that you put out to the world. It transmits the passion we feel toward what we are doing.

Another example is to think of your heart like a radio. It has many different stations. To tune into a station, you dial a specific frequency. As soon as you turn your attention to something (dial in on its frequency) you begin the journey of creating it. In the area where I live, if you tune to 94.7 you receive jazz music. If you tune into 94.5 you get rock music. If you tune to 102.4 you get classical. If you tune to 102.5 you get static.

Often times we are just slightly off frequency and wonder why we are not getting what we want. We get lost in the static, creating more static. We get what we focus on. To have whatever it is you want in your life—success, wealth, happiness, or whatever—you have to be sure you are on the right frequency. You have to be sure that you are in vibrational harmony with what you want. To be rid of something you do not want in your life, simply tune into a different frequency, the frequency of something you do want.

I see Cause and Effect as having four parts:

First, is getting very clear about what it is you want, why you want it, and then making a firm decision to have it. Without the decision firmly planted as a foundation, there is no need to go to the next step.

Second, is to raise your vibration until it matches what you want. In other words, own what you want in your heart even before you have it. Feel the passion. It's called connecting your head with your heart. It's called living in a dream fulfilled.

Third, is to trust by allowing what you want to come into your view without the feeling of needing to control the outcome.

Fourth, is letting go of fear and having faith.

It is usually part three and four that trips most people up. Letting go of all resistance, like fear or needing to control the outcome, and having faith that you can create what you're wanting can be challenging.

To win in a big way, you have to have trust and faith. You have to trust in yourself and the decisions you make. Then, you must have faith that something bigger than you will appear to support you in your endeavor. You may call it the subconscious, the super conscious, the source, the universe, coincidence, luck, the hidden force, God, Buddha, or whatever you choose to call it. It doesn't really matter. Whatever you choose to call it, have faith that the answers to your questions, the solutions to your problems, the contacts you need—whatever you may need to fulfill your dream—will come when the time is right.

Moving quickly and effortlessly toward your desired outcome is merely a process of using yourself and the world in a different way than what you are perhaps accustomed to. Moving toward your desired outcome requires allowing other new possibilities to exist. Even more than that, you must allow them to materialize and not try to force them into existence.

You must realize that you don't achieve your full potential and your dreams through your own efforts alone. Sheer willpower is not the answer. Yes, you do need willpower, and we will discuss that later. My point is that trying harder will not take you as far as you are capable of going. If you want to attain the success you desire, faster, you must take advantage of the support system that you cannot see.

Look at it as being in partnership. You provide the questions that need answers, and the vision of where you want to go—your invisible partner, the unseen power—will provide the answers.

Have faith and you will begin to see amazing things happen. The unseen force will operate through your intuition and will materialize in what seems to be luck or some sort of mystical phenomenon. You've had it happen. You are suddenly hit with an answer to a difficult problem in a moment of solitude. A solution may come to you in a dream or just as you are awakening, while all is quiet and you are relaxed. You have a flash of inspiration while you are mowing the grass and not thinking about business at all. You want to call someone, and you can't locate their number and suddenly you get a call from that person. We've all had that sort of thing happen and passed it off as a mere coincidence. Again, call it what you want or just accept it as a coincidence. It doesn't matter. Just accept it and know that there is more where that came from if you don't try to control all outcomes.

It's important to have a clear vision of what you want. Otherwise, the subconscious will operate in confusion, bringing you more confusion. That's why it's important to know exactly what you want and communicate it clearly so that you receive the correct support. Remember, you will gain support for whatever it is you communicate. That can be exciting or scary, depending on your point of view.

If you just back away and observe, you will be dazzled by what happens and the impact it has on your success, finances, and life. You can count on it. You don't even have to understand it. Just plug in with your trust and faith. Know that it is there, stay clear about what you want to accomplish, and watch it work for you. You don't have to understand how a radio wave works to tune in to a certain station do you? All you have to do is get good at tuning into the right station and it sends out the correct signal so that you receive the music you want. If you want wealth, be sure you are tuned into a wealth frequency. You always receive support and get back what you tune into. The question you should ask yourself often is, "What signal am I sending out?" Of course, that's easy to know. Just look at what you are receiving, and you'll know exactly what frequency you're putting out.

Do not approach your wealth casually, because a casual approach will always produce casualties.

WHAT YOU CAN ACCOMPLISH IS ONLY LIMITED BY YOUR IMAGINATION.

Nine

Will Power

"Success comes from you not at you."

--- Jim Britt

Making more money. Losing weight. Starting a business. Writing a book. Becoming debt free. Becoming wealthy. You can find the strategies to achieving anything you want to search for and come up with many solutions. In fact, as I mentioned before, if you want to become wealthy Google "becoming wealthy" and you get three billion, ninety-nine million files in .56 seconds. Yet every day, people continue to struggle to make money, lose weight, ease financial stress, and work a job they hate. Every day, they do the exact opposite of what they say they want to do. Why is that?

I call it, "The Law of Diminishing Intent."

Human beings have been starting and stopping projects, setting but not achieving goals, intending to/trying to become debt free, working toward financial independence, and not following through with their objectives, f-o-r-e-v-e-r. And they have a whole list of reasons why. Excuses really. And humans have been procrastinating forever!

The Law of Diminishing Intent is the state of acting against your better judgment through weakness of decision and willpower, even though you know better. It's when you do one thing even though you know you should be doing something else. It prevents entrepreneurs from succeeding in business, salespeople from making calls, writers from writing, coaches from coaching, and objectives from being reached.

I have good news and bad news for you. The bad news is that you are hardwired to be exactly as you are. In other words, your subconscious was programmed, much like the files in your computer, to be exactly who you are and to have what you have. Scary huh?

The good news is that you can change. Are you ready?

Again, the Law of Diminishing Intent is the state of acting against your better judgment through weakness of decision and the actions to follow. As humans, we always weigh out the pain associated with changing with the pain associated with staying where we are.

Example: A salesperson wants to earn more money and he or she *knows* that making more sales calls is the answer. They also know the pain associated with the feeling of being rejected when they get a 'no.' So, they weigh out the two pains and choose the lesser one. Then, they make up some excuse to justify why they didn't make the calls they said they would. Same can apply to anything you say you are going to accomplish; losing weight, starting a workout program, a new year's resolution, and so on.

Draw an almost complete circle on a page. Leave a small opening. A complete circle represents a firm decision to do something despite the pain. The opening represents an escape route, an excuse.

"You can't expect me to make sales calls in the rain?" Hey, last time I checked it rains on the successful too!

"Nobody is in after 3:00PM so it's not a good time to make calls." Last time I checked high achievers work after 3:00PM.

Don't you think it's in your best interest to learn how to strengthen and enforce your decisions over any form of behavioral or psychological weakness. If you want to become wealthy, the answer should be, "Yes!"

It's called willpower and letting go. So, what is this thing called willpower, and how do you use it to overcome the damaging effects of the Law of Diminishing Intent? Willpower and letting go are your superpowers if you use them to offset the larger pain of changing. Willpower is an undeniable commitment that you are going to succeed at something. It is the ability to give yourself a command, a direction, a target to hit, and then to do whatever it takes to hit it.

Letting go, on the other hand, is your ability to set aside those feeling, emotions, actions and behaviors that are not taking you in the direction you want to go. But, letting go also requires willpower. There is no command as great, nor any words as powerful, as the words "I will."

"I will do no less than whatever it takes to achieve my objective."

Again, if you have failed repeatedly at earning more money, when you decide to do it again, your subconscious offers you all the reasons why you failed in the past, and it happens in a split second, before you even have time to think about it.

The words "I will" sends a message to your subconscious telling it to override all previous programming to the contrary. It sends a message of tenacity, of winning over adversity, of courage over fear, of victory over defeat, and that you will persevere no matter what it takes.

The words "I will" are powerful.

> **I will** live the life I desire to live.
>
> **I will** lose the weight and get in shape.
>
> **I will** be debt free and financially independent.
>
> **I will** get through this obstacle, stronger and smarter.
>
> **I will** be defined by the life I want to live and not by my current circumstances.
>
> **I will** do no less than whatever it takes to accomplish my objectives.

Willpower is determined by the quality of, and the commitment to, the decisions you make. And remember, indecision is also a decision. It's a decision to stay right where you are. And with that decision, your willpower will do no less than wherever it takes to keep you there!

In the absence of willpower all the talents and great ideas in the world become worthless. You can start enforcing your willpower by letting go of those things that cause your intent to diminish.

Decide what you want, then execute! Then, let go of what doesn't support your desired outcome.

Don't allow your internal dialog to take over and pull you back into your current circumstances.

Let go of what doesn't support your desired outcome.

Michael Angelo was once asked how he sculpted such a beautiful sculpture of David. He said, quite simply, "I got a vision of what I wanted to create and simply chipped away what didn't fit my vision."

When it comes to execution, don't wait for the mood or feeling to hit you; that's nothing more than an excuse. You will accomplish nothing that way. If you are truly in it to win it, tell your subconscious that it's time to get to work. You create your mood! Don't wait for circumstances to take over and create it for you. Tell yourself that today will present both opportunities to advance your situation as well as obstacles that will test your willpower, but that you will move passed them. Therefore, mentally prepare yourself to jump on every opportunity to advance your position; determine in advance that nothing can stop you from reaching your objective.

I don't watch much football, but one day I caught the last quarter of Superbowl. I didn't even know who was playing. In the final two minutes, one team was ahead by only three points. Something fascinating hit me as I observed the team that was behind. It was the, 'No Huddle, Hurry Up Offense." In the past, I used to watch college football and I remember teams that employed this 1-2 punch tactic when they were losing the game and the clock was running down in the fourth quarter.

With pressure to score the tying or winning points in the last few minutes of the game, the offense rushes to the line of scrimmage without jumping into huddles between plays. The hope is to deliver a barrage of rapid knock-out blows which bewilder their opponent and ultimately score the needed points.

That day, watching the final few minutes of the game, I was amazed that the team deploying this tactic hadn't played particularly well in the minutes preceding. However, when the pressure is on and time is running out, and the stakes of losing are evident, through some divine inspiration, the offensive team was able to sync up and plowed down the field. The quarterback and receivers seemed mentally connected in some way. The team plowed down the field and made the winning touchdown!

The question that popped up in my mind was, "Why didn't they play like this the entire game? Why did they wait until the final few minutes to apply this tactic? And why was it that under extreme pressure they are able to employ the necessary plays to succeed? Why can't they play every minute of the game with the intensity of the, 'No Huddle, Hurry Up Offense?'" This approach doesn't always win the game, but they certainly played much better than they had the whole game.

Why not employ these tactics to your wealth building strategies? Do you play full out every day? Or, do you have a strategy plan to follow and when it comes to the end of the year, you are behind and rushing to complete projects? Is it when you finally realize you are behind that you employ the, "No Huddle, Hurry Up Offense? If so, why? Why do you procrastinate? Do you want to live your life that way? Do you want to put everything off until it is too late?

The difference between our lives and a football game is that neither of us are guaranteed our next plays. You and I aren't promised tomorrow. We could be in the third quarter of our lives and be taken out of the game at any time. We may never be able to finish our game.

Doesn't it just make sense then, to play full-out every moment of every day? Doesn't it make sense to employ your, "No Huddle, Hurry Up Offense" right now? I wonder how different your life would be if you approached it with this kind of intensity.

What if you cranked up your efforts and realized what's at stake? So, if your game ends short of the goal line, you can confidently pass to the next phase of life knowing you gave 100% of yourself and left everything on the playing field.

It's a challenging and courageous journey to take if you choose it. The work is mental and emotional. Great achievers have a crystal-clear vision of themselves accomplishing their dreams in their minds first. With this kind of clarity and focus you will be able to achieve the seemingly impossible.

Answer these questions: This is a powerful exercise!

> *What do you really want?*
>
> *Why do you want it?*
>
> *How do you know for sure you want it?*
>
> *Why don't you already have it?*
>
> *What does it feel like not having it?*
>
> *What's stopping you from having it?*
>
> *Why?*
>
> *What's at stake if you don't attain it?*

When you truly know the answers to these questions, you'll discover clarity of purpose that will guide you to focus on what's most important with certainty.

You don't have to wait until the last few minutes of the game to play full-out. It's about winning moment to moment. Why not play full-out so you can say you did everything you could.

Moments turn to hours, days, weeks, years, and in the end, a lifetime. What if you lived as *if* every evening was your last and every morning was your first?

Most people fail to achieve their goals, not because a lack of desire, but because of a lack of firm decision and willpower; that's why you must decide what you want, engage your willpower, let go of what doesn't support you, and then learn to put one determined foot in front of the other until you reach your destination.

The real question is, what are you focused on? Either you control your focus or your old subconscious programs will snatch it right away from you.

Every day take a sheet of paper and divide it down the middle from top to bottom. On the left side write down everything you did today. On the right side write down everything you could have done. Then look in the mirror and explain to yourself why you didn't do what you could have done.

We're living in a world where, unless you take ownership of your focus, you're in deep trouble…really deep trouble. More on this later.

Now is your time, your time to take the next step forward. It doesn't have to be a big step, but at least small consistent steps. Just start with one small step, then another. That's all you need to make progress. It's time to take ownership of what you want to accomplish and move toward it. What you choose to focus on with all your passion and willpower will, in fact, be created. You can watch it happen.

IT'S ALL YOURS IF YOU CHOOSE TO CONTROL WHAT YOU FOCUS ON. THAT'S JUST THE REALITY.

Ten

Your Hidden Wealth Talent

"You already possess the qualities you wish you had."

--- Jim Britt

Question: Do you really want to be wealthy?

Now, most people will quickly respond with, "Duh, of course!" to this question without giving it much consideration, but it should require some thought. As you know, there is a cost to everything you do, both in time and money. Achieving any significant goal always requires that we invest something of ourselves in the form of hard work and commitment. So, you say you want to be wealthy, but what are you willing to sacrifice to reach your goal?

Let me say that you can become as wealthy as you want. I know that's a pretty bold statement, but I'll say it again. You can be as wealthy as you want to be. It probably won't happen overnight or without some effort, unless you win the Lotto, but it can happen! Just like every other aspect of your life, being wealthy is a choice, not a twist of fate. You have the same resources available to you that every other wealthy person has used to build his or her fortune. Remember, it doesn't take a lot of money to make a lot of money. This is something worth remembering. It does take wealth, but not always money, to create wealth.

But first, let's look at the meaning of wealth.

Wealth simply means an abundance of something. Usually, when people use that word, and most often when I use the word, I'm referring to money. But it can also mean an abundance of anything else important to you: freedom, health, family, talent, peace of mind. These are all forms of wealth that are just as important as money. In fact, without these other kinds of wealth, getting rich would not be a very happy place.

But what's interesting is that by drawing on other forms of wealth, you can create monetary wealth that much faster, and it will be a far more rewarding process.

You see, we all hold an immense fortune inside us that can be channeled to create monetary wealth. I call this your "hidden wealth talent," because most people don't understand the vast potential they have to become as wealthy as they want to be.

What is your hidden wealth talent? It's your time, talents, passions, dreams, desires, values, and core beliefs. Your hidden wealth talent is your passion and vision for the world and how you can contribute to it. Your hidden wealth talent are the things that make you truly happy. Your hidden wealth talent is also your mindset about becoming wealthy. You can unlock this hidden wealth talent merely by first identifying it, then focusing it. That is, first figure out what it is about you that makes you unique and special, then decide how these things can lead you to becoming wealthy.

Someone once said, and I'm not sure who that someone is, that if we divided all of the money in the world equally between every man, woman, and child, we'd each have more than a million dollars. But, they also said that in a very short period of time most of that money would be back in the same hands before the division took place— the ones whom had discovered their hidden wealth talent.

Well, I'll tell you a little wealth secret. The way to true riches has always been through focusing on our hidden wealth talent. Using their hidden wealth talent, people who started life in the worst and most poverty-stricken conditions have become some of the richest and most famous people in the world.

Using your hidden wealth talent effectively is a sure signal that financial wealth will follow. And the best thing is, you don't need any special intelligence or education.

I once had a talk with a young man who had an MBA degree from USC. At one point in the conversation, he told me that his car was going belly up, and he couldn't afford to buy another one.

He said, "The worst part is, I keep seeing all these people driving around in BMWs and living in big homes, wearing fine cloths, and

I know I'm at least as smart, or maybe even smarter than they are. So why am I not driving a car like that?" He said, "In fact, I have a neighbor that drives a $100K Mercedes, and he didn't even finish high school. I don't get it."

I said, "The answer is quite simple. Your neighbor has tapped into their hidden wealth talent, while you have not. And that's their ultimate advantage. They may not be as educated, and they may not even work as hard as you, yet they have discovered their hidden wealth talent and put it to work."

This idea got my friend's attention. He had never been very interested in my financial advice, until now. After all, I am a high school dropout that drives one of those luxury cars. However, immediately, he wanted to brain-storm.

Currently he worked for an organization that promoted large events around the country, a job he landed right after graduating college. His job was making sure all events were set up properly. He actually made a fairly decent salary, but he wasn't very happy with the job he was doing day-to-day.

Interestingly enough, though, with a little more questioning, his real interest lay in two areas. The entertainment field was one. He had passion for playing the rock guitar and toyed with the idea of joining a band on the weekends. He also had a long-standing passion for public speaking.

By the time we said goodbye, he was already focusing his mind on how he might put his hidden wealth talent to work for himself. And the next time we talked, he was happy to report some success!

Keeping his interests in mind, and doing some homework, he approached his boss with an idea for one of their upcoming events having a rock-n-roll theme. He was actually able to get a big-name band to play at the event at a reduced cost and a well-known National speaker (me) to commit to the project as their keynote speaker. He was given the go-ahead to proceed and the event was a huge success. The keynote speaker even gave him some tips for breaking into the speaking business.

The success of this event influenced his boss to promote him to produce additional such events. And to top it off, it was a higher-paying position and less hours.

A few months later, he started delivering speeches to local meet-ups to develop his speaking talents and material. And he got there driving the new Infinity he wanted so much.

A couple years later, he is being paid for delivering keynote speeches. The money is rolling in, and he's now shopping for a new home.

It's funny how people's perceptions can change. He later told me that the nice cloths, cars, and homes weren't what he really wanted. His real fulfillment came from using his hidden talent to really prosper.

So, what is your hidden wealth talent? Do you know? Do you want to know? Tapping into your hidden wealth talent is not a minor matter.

Expressing your hidden wealth talent in the world may involve a number of big changes in your life that you have to be willing to make. But financial wealth, if you don't have it, will never come without change. And it starts with changing your perception of wealth, your mental programming, and discovering your hidden wealth talent. If that weren't true, if we didn't have to change our habits and mental programming to become wealthy, then we'd all be wealthy!

The reality is, it's also possible to accumulate a great deal of money by making only minor changes in your life and lifestyle.

What if you got really serious about creating a fortune for yourself and your family? What if you became totally focused on building a legacy of contribution in world? What if you focused on money enough to become financially independent? And most importantly, what if you created this new financial wealth by simply utilizing the hidden wealth talent you already possess?

Imagine, then, the power of making bigger changes and using your talent to create even more money. You'll get richer faster, and the best part of all is that, when you're getting wealthy by expressing your inner passions in the world, you will be happier by default! In fact, the money you gain will be secondary to the joy of living your life and the satisfaction that you are doing something that is personally fulfilling.

Most people live their lives in quiet desperation when it comes to money and happiness, hoping that someday things will get better. But the reality is that it won't, unless you are willing to do something about it.

FOR CIRCUMSTANCES TO CHANGE, YOU HAVE TO MAKE CHANGES.

Eleven

What ALL Wealthy People Have in Common

"We cannot discover the truth if we insist that we already know it. When we admit that we do not know, that very realization opens a place for it."

--- Jim Britt

What's the secret to incredible financial success? The secret is, there is no <u>one</u> secret! The reality is, there are many secrets that work together in combination with one another, giving you the winning combination to succeed! Think of success like a giant vault at the bank with a thick steel door blocking it and a combination lock. Unless you have the right combination to that lock, it doesn't matter how much you beat on the door, how hard you work, how many lists you make or good intentions you have, because there is a combination you must know to unlock that door and get it to swing open so you can walk through to the other side. In this chapter, I'll be sharing a couple of those success secrets with you—some straight-talk keys that make the difference between struggling your whole life in frustration or becoming wealthy.

Many years ago, I met a very wealthy person and I asked what inspired him to be wealthy? His answer really surprised me.

"Money is a game and the man with the most notches on his belt wins." I was shocked! I was a young man at the time, and having grown up without much, I wanted to become rich. Yet after hearing this person's response, I looked deeper into his eyes and frankly, he didn't seem all that happy and I sensed a lack of balance in his life. He was out of shape and had a look in his eyes of anxiety, loneliness, and anger. I could tell that he had stepped on a lot of people to get to where he was.

How about you? Do you think that being wealthy takes putting yourself first and trampling over those that get in your way? Do you think that being wealthy means putting the lust for money ahead of everything else?

I've also met very wealthy people who give back to their community, have large circles of friends, and always seemed to be abundant in so many other ways.

In fact, a year or so ago I took a camera crew around the country and interviewed eleven self-made mega millionaires and one billionaire. The requirement was that they all had to have started with nothing. In other words, they didn't inherit their wealth. And all twelve made their money in different industries: internet marketing, traditional business, real estate, television, direct sales, social media, etc. If you asked any of these twelve individuals the same question, you'd likely get this sort of answer: "Wealth is simply a vehicle that magnifies your deeper personality traits and mindset."

If you are a good person, and have access to resources, such as high achievers, it will only make you a better one. If your nature is negative, it will also magnify your unhealthy attributes on the downside, and you will find yourself hanging around others that will support you in your negativity.

The following is what I have learned from my own experiences and the experiences of these twelve mega-millionaires, as well as others I have associated myself with over the past forty years.

Wealth is the ultimate power of leverage. Nothing is truer about becoming, and deciding to become, wealthy. It is a magnifying glass into your mindset.

I have tried to model myself after this philosophy, never forgetting that money is simply a means to achieving larger and greater things in life. After all, if the only reason you are pursuing buckets of money is to swim in it like Uncle Scrooge, you may find yourself the richest person in a very unhappy world.

Wouldn't it be nice if you could simply decide to become wealthy and you did?

Well, let me fill you in on a big secret...YOU CAN!

You already know the basics. You know that you should pay off your debt and start budgeting. You know that all you need to do is regularly invest money into your savings and let time do the work. Spend less, save more, build your investment portfolio…you've heard it time and time again. Then why aren't you on the way to becoming wealthy?

There are many reasons that people don't take action, even though they have the information. The reality is that so many people are just simply afraid to change. Fear takes a lot away from a person. They don't want to fail, but when you buy into fear it will take you down that path.

Here's one key: for things to change for you financially, you have to make a change, otherwise you'll continue to keep producing the same results you've been producing. This may come as a shock to you, but most people really don't want to change. Just give them a beer, point them toward the sofa, and give them the television remote and some potato chips. They will continue to complacently live out their lives, complaining about what they don't have.

Most people are much too busy earning a living to become financially free. They spend the majority of their time focused on what they *don't have* and what they *don't want*, on how to pay the bills, instead of focusing on what they *do have* and what they *do want* in their lives.

I know people, as I'm sure you do, that love having the drama of being up to their ears in debt. It's a balance beam that keeps excitement in their lives. It's a roller coaster ride that is thrilling but always drops them off at the same place time and time again. But at such a huge cost! What they don't realize is that they can't maintain their balance or thrill forever. At some point, you have to decide where to get off…or you fall off.

I've often wondered, as I'm sure you have, why two people with the very same background and experience in the same type of business can have two very different outcomes—one gains wealth, while the other barely survives. What determines the difference between someone who earns $50,000, $500,000 and someone who earns

$5,000,000 a year? Is it their education, their experience, the amount of money they have already, or is it simply a lucky break?

One of the things I discovered in my forty plus-year career is that successful people do things in a different way. To put it yet another way, they do things that the majority of people are not willing to do. Most have been conditioned to believe that creating wealth is difficult, or that it's only for the lucky few. What do you believe?

Everyone wants greater financial success, but the statistics say that most will never have it. Get this…this is shocking! According to the U.S. Social Security Administration, the average retired couple has less than $7,000 in savings. At retirement, 45% will depend on extra money from relatives for their survival. 30% depend on charity. 20% will still be working, and only 5% will be self-sustaining.

Wow! I don't know about you, but I find this unbelievable and even frightening!

I'm sure that people never believe, or even think, this would ever happen to them, but statistics say, it will! So, according to statistics, at age 65 there is a 90% chance you'll still be working for someone else and with no nest egg to retire or depending on relatives to survive. I don't think people plan for this to happen. No one in their right mind would make a plan like that. They simply don't have a plan for it *not* to happen. They convince themselves that *someday* they are going to be a success, to start their own business, to make a financial plan for their future, to have all they want in life…someday.

Someday...what an interesting concept. Think of all the things that were supposed to have happened by now, all those things that you may have convinced yourself were just around the corner. To most, that *someday* is where we've convinced ourselves we would be right now if only we had more time, more talent, more education, more money, or maybe a better opportunity available.

How about you? Is your level of financial success today where you thought it would be five years ago? Before going any further, I would urge you to stop right now and take a realistic look at your last five years. Have you truly made progress? Are the last five years what *you* wanted? Are you where you thought you'd be today? And, most importantly, do you have a solid plan for the next five?

You and I both know that there are no guarantees in life, but I'm going to suggest what you've probably already concluded; for things to change in your life, you have to make a change. I want to help you to make the changes necessary to have all you want in life.

Too many people like to complain, but just don't want to make the effort. They don't have time. They'll do it next year. Let me tell you, you have to find time to get your financial situation in order if you want to gain wealth. Time is costing you money. The more time you spend trying to pay off credit cards, the more you pay the credit card company and contribute to their wealth.

I'm not saying to ignore your financial obligations. What I'm saying is that paying off your credit cards, although a good place to start, will not bring you wealth. Why? Because after you pay them off you are still left with the mentality that charged them to the max in the first place.

Don't let denial, fear, laziness, procrastination, or a need for drama get in the way of your wealth plan. You *can* have all the money you want. It just takes learning and developing the traits that rich people use, and some time to make it happen. The pathway to wealth is something you can absolutely choose to take.

To become wealthy, you will need some vital traits. Let me offer you a few.

First, is a firm decision to become wealthy. Wealthy people make solid decisions and commit to seeing them through. Those who are not financially successful put off decisions or mess around with their decision once it is made.

The first step in becoming wealthy, whatever wealth means to you, is making the decision to become wealthy; a decision that doesn't allow for anything less. Mediocrity is not an option to the wealthy. A decision creates a mindset, and a mindset makes you as mechanical and predictable as a calculator. Hit this number and it appears on the screen. Better yet, decide on a number and it appears in your bank account. It's really surprising though how many people don't like to make decisions. They do all sorts of things to keep the moment of decision at arms-length including not thinking about the decision, fretting over who the decision might offend, worrying about the resources needed to pull off the decision, or hoping they'll just get lucky and make the money they need without making a decision. All excuses for not making the decision.

The real problem is that most are stuck in a comfort zone and making a decision would possibly mean having to do something different that might be a bit painful. That's an obstacle we all face—the pain of staying stuck in our current situation or the pain of change. Most people would rather live with the old for fear that becoming the new is too painful.

They say that the greatest instinct humans have is survival. I disagree. I believe our greatest instinct is to stay the same. We stay the same for fear of the pain associated with changing.

Let's say a person makes the decision to be wealthy. What happens when the old programs, the old habit patterns, and mind chatter kicks in? "Wait a minute! What makes you think you have the talent to become wealthy? I've never done it before! Maybe I really can't become wealthy. I don't have the expertise, time, money, etc. To become wealthy." And before long all the self-talk has pulled you off course and changed the decision (that you never really made in the first place) into something totally different from becoming wealthy. Sound familiar? We all do it to some degree.

Remember this: <u>every income level requires a different you</u>. You have to be willing to let go of the "old you" and embrace the challenge of becoming the "new you." And if you want to learn, grow, and change, you have to hang around people that challenge you to become better. If you want to become a million-dollar-a-year earner, but you hang around and take input from people earning $60,000 a year, you'll likely to be right where they are financially. If you want to become a million-dollar-a-year earner, *you have to make a decision to change*, and then you have to hang around million-dollar-a-year earners. Otherwise, there will always be somebody offering you the wrong input and telling you how to run your life, making you feel insecure and doubtful.

I know people, as I'm sure you do, who go to work every day to a job they hate. They hate what they earn and/or what they do, but they stay because they feel they have no other choice. They justify their position by calling it 'job security.' But what they don't realize is that there is no security in a job! It's called *prolonged poverty* in my book!

It's like living in a place you hate, but you're afraid to move because of your job. Then you lose your job and can't afford to move, so you look for another insecure position that will keep you in the place you hate. That's a sort of insanity, don't you think?

What would I say to a person in that position? "If you want to get better, you have to make better decisions, and you have to hang out with and take input from those who've done it." I would say "If you want to be rich, you have to stop working for someone else's goals and dreams and make a decision to start working for your own. You have to stop with the employee mentality and start thinking like wealthy people think." So, the next time you catch yourself saying, "I have no choice," stop and ask yourself if that's really true.

Here's the key: it is your job to make the decision, one that doesn't allow for anything less. It's not your job to figure out how you will attain wealth until the decision is made. Your initial job is to make a firm decision. Up until the decision is made, nothing happens— except, of course, the decision to stay where you are now. In reality, not making a decision is a decision to leave everything status quo.

Let me ask you a question. Let's say that there are two components that make up 100% of your financial success. Those two components are "decision" and "opportunity, or financial vehicle." My question is this: what percentage do each play in your financial success? When I ask a group this question, some say 50/50. Some say 80/20 and others say 20/80. What do you think? Here's the answer. It's 100% decision and 0% vehicle. Because without a firm decision, the vehicle doesn't matter in the least. Because without the decision, there will be no success no matter what the vehicle. In fact, without the decision to become wealthy, there is no reason to even search for the vehicle. That would be like shopping for something that you have no interest in having.

Rich people develop the skill of making the best decision possible with the best information possible in the timeliest manner possible. They are quick to decide and quick to take responsibility for their decisions, positive or negative.

The next trait all wealthy people have in common is that they are bold. Financially successful people have learned that action is vital. And often times, that requires a level of boldness. They know that procrastination kills. They live with the reality of consequences and know there will always be uncertainty in decisions, but they boldly step forward and make the decision anyway.

No one can see all possible ramifications; no one can predict every contingency; no one can absolutely prevent failure. The wealth minded person knows that failure is not final; it's just one of those possible outcomes that happens on their way to success.

The real danger surrounding decision making is not, "Will I make the wrong decision?" Instead, it is, "Did I make the best decision possible given the facts and circumstances?" Success minded individuals invest in learning what they need to make the correct decisions from those who have done what they want to do.

But, when it comes to investing in mentorship, so often I hear people say, "I can't afford it. It costs too much." When in reality, they can't afford not to, because it will cost you dearly if you don't. Wealthy people look at value, not cost. What will the investment make them, or make of them, rather than what it will cost them?

The success minded, bold person, will always recover from poor decisions; they know that they'll learn and become wiser. The meek minded will mess around and miss opportunities, saying, "I don't have the time. I don't have the money. The timing is not right, etc." And when they finally do make a decision, chances are their decision will have no momentum, no passion, and no urgency.

If you wait for everything to be right before you decide, chances are you'll miss the opportunity all together.

The real question is, "What do you really want?" Are you like most everyone who is obsessed with success, with having more money, more things, and better futures for themselves and their family?

Are you intrigued by the top companies: success stories of rags to riches, who's the coolest, the hottest, the richest, the boldest? Are you just dreaming about success or standing on the sidelines observing other people's successes and wishing you had what they have? Do you justify why you aren't financially successful? Or are you bold enough to step out in the spotlight and take center stage before you have all the answers?

The real questions are: "Do you want to be rich? Do you want to retire wealthy? What would financial success look like to you?" Most people have never defined what financial success would be for them, and they've never made the decision to have it. And that's the only reason they don't have it! The most important question that you can ask yourself is, "Have I defined what financial success means to me, or am I just working for someone else's success and letting them define my level of financial worth?" Or are you basing your future financial success on past experiences? How you answer that question can change your life!

Often times, there is a feature in the investment section of the Sunday newspaper. It's a success story column on people who've made it big financially in a respective business. You can also find those stories in magazines like Entrepreneur or Inc. You'll find stories of individuals who have carved out a niche for themselves in selected fields, lived a fulfilled life serving others with their skills, and amassed quite a fortune while doing so. You'll always find one common trait in all the featured personalities. Not one of them. Not some of them. But this trait is in all of them! It's called a "wealth mindset." Despite the fact that they're from different backgrounds, all of them possess the same mindset when it comes to money. Wealthy people think differently. This is the infamous "money consciousness" that most of the motivational and personal development trainers speak of so often in their books and seminars.

This wealthy mindset basically means this:

Regardless of the physical condition that you may be currently in, as long as you see yourself bathing in financial abundance, your actions will maneuver and circumstances will unfold in a way to create the wealth that you see yourself enjoying. If you possess the wealthy mindset, you will have the Midas touch when it comes to earning money. If you don't, you won't. That simple. The fortunate thing is that all of us possess the innate ability to fire up this wealthy mindset. But the key is letting go of the old you and holding true to the new you that you want to become. First is making the decision to be wealthy. Second is being bold. Next, is letting go of your limiting beliefs about money.

Some people frown at the mere mention of money. How many times have you heard people say something like this: "Oh, I'm not doing this for the money" or "Money isn't everything." Well, they're not wrong. Money isn't everything. The fact is that money in itself has no value. It's the things that money can buy when in circulation that makes it so valuable. Money can buy material possessions, personal freedom, peace of mind, and we all deserve to have what we want.

At the same time, if you look from a different angle, once you've got enough money to be financially free, it can literally change what you do from laborious work to spending more precious moments with your family and friends, as well as doing the things you love.

Money can also allow you to contribute to a charity and benefit the less privileged.

On the other end of the scale, some people tend to overvalue the importance of money so much so that they become slaves to it. They love money so much that they let this passion cause their downfall; we've all witnessed it.

In essence, if you never come to terms with what money can bring forth into your life, its real value, your uneasiness with the "idea" of money will limit your ability to attract more of it. To put it simply, just imagine this: would you go into a car showroom if you never had the intention to purchase a car? You may not want to buy it now, but the fact that you walked into the showroom implies that you appreciate the value of what a car brings. It can serve as a means of transportation for you and your family. And, because of the perceived value you see in owning a car, you'll find the ways and means to get one. Having money is the same. Once you see its value and believe you can have it, you'll find the ways and means to get it.

Remember, you can't create something that you're not in harmony with or that you haven't decided to have. Therefore, it becomes imperative that before you move onto other steps to really get this wealthy mindset concept, you should definitely have a conversation with yourself, or someone that can mentor you, to let go of the beliefs that are limiting you about money.

Having money means: (finish the sentence for yourself)

What came up? Do you feel your answer will move you toward being wealthy?

Answer these questions:

Why do you deserve to be wealthy?

What do you believe about money?

How did you come to believe this?

Who taught you to believe that way?

Were they wealthy?

Who taught them?

The only way to change a belief is to challenge it. A belief is something that you have decided is true; though, it may not be at all. A belief is simply an opinion that something is true. The good news is that you can change a belief simply by changing your decisions and letting go of the old you.

If you want to be wealthy, you have to first decide to be wealthy. Whatever being wealthy means to you. Next is to decide why you want to be wealthy. What's the payoff for wealth? Your 'why' is the fuel that will take you where you want to go. It's the passion behind the decision.

Everyone has the right to be wealthy. YOU have the right to be wealthy; and yet, most allow a temporary lack of money to eat into their minds, literally confining them into the vicious cycle of mediocrity.

The bottom line is that people are poor because they have not yet decided to be wealthy. To put it another way, mediocre earners are mediocre earners because they have decided to be. They resonate with mediocrity.

So long as you make a conscious decision to become wealthy, and have utmost faith that you can achieve it while letting go of outdated beliefs about money, you will act accordingly to what you believe. Why not say "yes" to getting wealthy today! And say it with conviction.

Deciding to be wealthy only gets you started on the quest, but what sustains you throughout the journey is the 'why' you want to be wealthy and letting go of the mind chatter that pulls you back into your old habit patterns.

What is the reason that you want an extra $1 million in your bank account, or you want to earn a million dollars a year? Why do you want to work your butt off, sacrificing your weekends to work a business or a job that only allows you to get by financially, when there is so much more available to you?

If you do not have a burning desire supporting your decision, and you don't let go of your old way of thinking and believing, you'll find your inspiration tapering off sooner and your decision fading into something totally different from being wealthy.

That's the trap that most everyone falls into.

Try this exercise. Take a piece of paper and scribble down all the reasons you can think of about why you want to be wealthy. Maybe you'd like to retire earlier and travel around the world? Or you want to quit your job and be a full-time parent? Write down as many why's as you can think of. Needless to say, the one that resonates with the deepest part of your heart should be written on an index card to remind you of the outcome you desire.

You'll also want to determine what wealth is to you. How much you want will inadvertently determine the action you'll need to set forth to reach it.

Wealth can be whatever you say it is. For some, it might mean 10 million in the bank. For others it might mean having enough residual income coming monthly to completely cover your overhead. For example, if it's $5,000 per month that you're looking for, working in your existing job and going for a raise in pay might suffice. However, if $100,000 per month is what you intend to achieve, other alternatives such as starting your own business, investing in properties, or working on your skills sets to better serve the marketplace will probably be more effective. More importantly, knowing how much you want prepares your mind for the potential issues you may face to make that happen.

The challenge therefore becomes: How do you know how much you want?

Arbitrarily quoting a figure will probably do you more harm than good. If the amount you pull out of the sky is much higher than what you really want, your approach to acquire the wealth may not be in harmony with your "why," and you may end up burning yourself out. In the event that the amount is lesser than what you really want, then you'll find yourself re-adjusting your "why" which may not inspire you to keep going. Again your "what" your "why" and your "mindset" need to be in harmony.

Determining how much you want doesn't have to be rocket science. You can do this by taking into consideration the objective for what you want the wealth for, your "why." Do an analysis of the costs necessary to sustain it. Let's say, for example, that your reason is to provide your family with a comfortable lifestyle which includes oversees travel for vacations twice a year, along with being debt free. You can include the costs of paying off your debt, traveling overseas for holiday twice a year, and your comfortable living expenses into your analysis.

A lot of people think having a wealthy mindset involves only constantly thinking about getting rich. That's not it at all. The most important element is to make the decision, then not obsess about how to do it. Take action and allow it to unfold. Play the "what if" game. Brainstorm possibilities. Be open to solutions. Expose your mind to possibilities, to new opportunities. Let go of your fears. Discuss with a qualified mentor or coach.

Suppose you want to get from point "A" to point "B." There's route 1, route 2, 3 all the way to infinity. When you believe that there's only one way to get there, it limits your possibilities. When you are totally open to how to get there, the mind starts considering many options and may prompt you to act on the one that you hadn't even thought of before. Along the way, your wealthy mindset may allow you to recognize different opportunities, encouraging you to change course and go through a totally different experience than originally planned.

I remember one entrepreneur I knew attained wealth in a totally different manner than expected. Initially, his plan was to market his own music compositions through conventional methods. But, he instead stumbled upon online internet marketing and embarked on an unconventional route to becoming an internet millionaire. It was not an easy route as he had to juggle learning about the new internet marketing model, of which he knew nothing about, while still working a full-time job. But his burning desire to be rich got him through the hurdle to financial freedom.

Start to imagine yourself as already having wealth. Before you physically acquire the wealth that you've envisioned, you need to own it as if you already possess the amount of money you desire! How would you feel right now if you were wealthy? What would you be doing differently? How would your life be different? How would your day unfold? Start to own the result of your wealth now! The subconscious mind is unable to differentiate between actual possession and mere visualization. So, by imagining that you already have it, you're encouraging your subconscious mind to seek ways to transform your imaginary feelings into the real thing.

I know many people refute this type of thinking as impractical. But if you think about it, isn't everything around us a true manifestation of someone else's imagination? Everything man made was in someone's imagination before it was created. And when they possessed the passion to create it, the ways and means appeared. The Wright brothers imagined being able to fly and the reality is, we are now able to fly in an airplane from one country to another in a matter of hours. Thomas Edison imagined lighting the whole room using a single source and as a result, the light bulb was invented! Yes, it took a few tries, but eventually he created it.

Look around right now. If you are in a room, look at all the things in that room that made someone wealthy. Why not you? Take a walk outside and look around. How many things do you see that made some else wealthy? Why not you? It all started in someone's imagination. They owned it first in their mind before it became a reality. It's a fact that without the imagination of great visionaries, we would not be able to enjoy many things that we enjoy today. Radio, television, automobiles and thousands of other great inventions would not be present today if not for someone first imagining it into existence. Vision comes first, then the answers!

You too possess the same capability to create; improve your own destiny by constructing it in your mind first. All improvement in your life begins in the improvement in your mental pictures. Change your mental pictures and you change the outcome of your life, like changing a channel on TV.

So how do you build this imagination? Jack Nicklaus calls it, 'going to the movies.' That's easy and fun to apply. He's known in the industry to have a very clear picture of how he should play the game before actually going into one. He visualizes an outcome before starting the game. He sees himself winning! In his own words, he states, "I never hit a shot, not even in practice, without having a very sharp, in-focus picture of it in my mind first. First, I see the ball where I want it to fall, nice and white and sitting up high, easy to hit, on the green grass. Then, the scene quickly changes, and I see the ball going there; its path, trajectory and shape, and even how it lands. Then, there is a sort of fade out and the next scene shows me making the kind of swing that will turn the previous images into reality." You and I can do the same. For example, you can imagine receiving income checks when you open the mailbox every day. Or you can picture yourself receiving an award for being nominated the best entrepreneur in your country or having a best-selling book. Not only does it send the message to your subconscious, it serves as a great form of daily inspiration.

Okay, lets come in for a landing …

It is absolutely essential to have a crystal-clear picture of what you want to accomplish before you begin. If you want to attain wealth, you must learn to operate with a sharply defined mental image of the outcome you want to attain.

Focus your attention on the spot where you want to land, not on where you are now, or on any misconceptions or shortcomings you may think you have. In other words, visualize your arrival and you'll develop a magnetic harmony with the ways and means required to get there. With a clear mental image, you'll attract the people and circumstances needed to get you where you want to go. Solutions will begin to appear, and obstacles will seem to disappear. Answers will come to you. People will show up to support you in your endeavor. Look at the end result as something that you are already prepared to do, you just haven't done it yet.

You have the potential, and the resources are available for you to have anything you want. The only thing missing is your firm, unshakable decision, the wealth mindset and letting go of your old way of thinking and believing.

Think about this. Your success is something that you have been preventing; it's not something you have to struggle to make happen. You can't force anything into existence. All you can do is step out of the way and let it unfold. The critical key is to not let fear, doubt, other people, or mind chatter push your success away.

You'll find that the solutions taking you toward your goals will come to you in the most unexpected and sudden ways when you let go of the old you and embrace the new you.

You don't need the *perfect* plan first. What you need is a *perfectly* clear decision about your success and the right mindset and the ideal way to get you there will materialize. You can't get all the answers up front before the decision is made, so don't waste your time trying.

The success formula doesn't involve getting everything neatly organized, with everything in its proper place and sequence and all the risks eliminated before you make the move. If you want that, then get a 9-5 job. But realize that will never make you wealthy.

If you want to be a wealthy entrepreneur you have to sometimes shoot from the hip, going into new territory and charting the map as you go. Be willing to cope with confusion for a while and shape your plan as you go. Allow some disorder, and then create order out of it. If you get too detailed in the beginning, you'll find yourself worrying over potential problems and non-productive details, instead of what's really important, which is getting the job done. Get a target, point, then take action!

Your true greatness lies within your ability to decide what you want and commitment to having it, and then taking bold action to get it. Develop your mindset, then imagine it into existence.

You've heard the saying "think outside the box!" Here's my version: "Don't ever get in the box!" The world you have perceived in the past is the world you now live in. The world you perceive now is the world you will create in the future. And the world you create is limited only by your imagination, your mindset, and your ability to let go of the old you. Create your vision, then stand back and allow your conviction to decide the quality of your life and the degree of your wealth!

Everyone has the right to be wealthy. You have the right to be wealthy. Yet, most allow a temporary lack of money to eat into their minds, literally confining them into the vicious cycle of mediocrity. The bottom line is that people are poor because they have not yet decided to be rich. So long as you make a conscious decision to become wealthy and have the utmost faith that you can achieve it, you will act accordingly to what you believe. We all create our own reality, abundant or not. A person who believes that the universe is abundant, and that they can attain whatever level of financial success they desire, and a person who believes that money only comes from working hard and will receive money only from hard work, are both right. Each will have many experiences to prove that their "belief" about abundance is "fact."

The good news is though…

YOU CAN CHANGE YOUR BELIEF, AND THEREFORE CHANGE WHAT YOU EXPERIENCE.

Twelve

The Predator and the Prey

"Self-defeat in any endeavor doesn't mean that victory doesn't exist. It simply means that you approached it incorrectly."

--- Jim Britt

Maybe you have dreams and goals, but somehow things are simply not moving in the direction you had planned. Or worse, maybe you've stopped believing that the life you've always wanted is even attainable.

Let me ask you, do you see similarities between you and your parents? The reality is that DNA passes down through generations— you, your parents, grandparents, great-grandparents, and so on. You could actually track it right back to when your ancestors lived in a cave. And in order to survive, prehistoric man needed to be able to see an event and interpret it as danger or safe immediately! They had two dominant thoughts, "Kill something to eat" and "keep from being killed and eaten." And to some degree, we still have this mechanism of recognition in place today. We just don't view it the same way.

Something happens, and your brain instinctively stretches and searches all through your past networks, or dendrites—which are the memory channels woven throughout your DNA—looking to match some sort of pattern so you can make an instant decision. Is this safe or is it dangerous? The meaning you give something is based upon a constant comparison of your past experiences and DNA programming projected into the future with the anticipation or possibility of it happening again. Something happens and you immediately tell yourself a story about what it means. Remember, it's a made-up story in your mind. It's not real… yet.

So when you step into the future, you don't really step into an empty future, but rather into a future that is filled with interpretations about what happened in the past, and what could happen in the future if you proceed.

For example, a salesperson prepares her presentation. She is excited for that important appointment to make a sale, but instead of a sale, she gets a very rude "no." Now, at the next presentation, she won't step into a blank future, but rather, she'll step into a negative past experience. Put enough of these "no's" together and now the salesperson does everything in her power to avoid prospecting, so she doesn't have to experience another 'no.' Again, the rejection had no meaning until she gave it one. She got a "no" and made it mean something about her, when in reality it wasn't about her at all.

Imagine three circles. A circle on the left. In that circle something happens to you—broken marriage, lose money in a business venture, etc. You decide what goes in there. Now there's the circle on the right. This is where you gave what happened to you meaning. Examples: bad experience with last business. Business didn't work last time and may not work now. Marriage ended in divorce. I don't want that again. You gave whatever happened to you a meaning.

Now, the circle on bottom. You live your life as if your story is true. We live in a black and white world. However, most live their life in the gray as if their story is true, when in reality, it's a made-up story created from past experiences. This is an example of inauthentic living. You are living as if your story is true and reacting accordingly. Everyone has a story, but the reality is that your story is in large part an illusion; it's a made-up belief. All beliefs are false until you decide they are true, but that doesn't make them true. But if you decide it is true, then it will be true for you.

Core beliefs work like sunglasses. Sunglasses change incoming light before it hits our eyes. The world does not change to a shaded image just because you put on sunglasses. No, really! Only your perception changes looking through the glasses. Wear sunglasses long enough and you will eventually forget you have them on.

That's how beliefs work as well. Believe something long enough and eventually you experience it as true. It then becomes a core belief. Core beliefs change how you see the world before you are even aware of seeing anything. Core beliefs also determine how the world sees you. That's right. The world sees you the way you see you.

On the other hand, this mechanism is critical for your survival because it separates things that might get you killed and eaten from everything else. In a sense, your core beliefs protect you. But not always, because you automatically filter everything that happens to you according to core beliefs, which may or may not be true. In other words, your core beliefs may not be taking you in the direction you want to go.

Prey animals cannot afford to not follow their core beliefs. Humans are no exception. The top priority your brain has is to keep you from getting killed and eaten—maybe not literally in today's world, but you get the idea. You may fear getting killed and eaten by an audience when you step on a stage, or by a prospect when making a presentation.

These things represent predators waiting to invade your refuge and attack you if you leave yourself open or start to take a risk. Our brains are wired to fear monsters, noises, and dangerous situations, because that is what our ancestors had to do to survive.

Humans of all ages establish and stick to routines no matter what, so they can survive. We take comfort in our routines. This makes perfect sense. For example, if a predator attacks at dusk, then its prey should be out and about during the day and asleep and out of reach at night. If a predator attacks at noon, then the prey would most likely be nocturnal. Sticking to this routine helps the prey stay alive. Our prey habits are all about avoiding predators, discomfort, or dangerous situations.

Humans are prey animals whose top priority is not getting killed and eaten, avoiding pain, or not getting hurt. We therefore form habits to help us survive, and then stick to those habits no matter how inconvenient, uncomfortable, unrealistic, or awful they are. We've learned over countless generations that straying from our routine puts us at risk. Our brain does everything in its power to keep that from happening. This is why people refuse to change until the pain of *not* changing is worse than the pain of changing.

We desire change, but when faced with the pain of change we weigh out both sides—the pain of staying where we are versus the pain associated with changing. Whatever causes us less pain is what wins out. But the question is, do you win, or do you continue living a life of more of the same?

Core beliefs form our entire reality from birth to death unless we take action to change them. The good news is that you can change your beliefs. We do it all the time. Remember, a belief is a made-up story. Want to change it, make up something new!

It's like earning a six-figure income, for example. Once you hit it, it becomes a core belief, so you settle for nothing less. The catch is that changing your beliefs will force you to confront programming that your brain interprets as being essential for your very survival. This is why crash diets, New Year's resolutions, joining a gym, opening a savings account, cutting up the credit cards, and other drastic changes rarely last more than a few days to a few weeks. At some point, the desire for change surrenders to the brain's built-in attempts to keep you from getting killed and eaten.

How do you change a core belief? Make up something new, let go of all that doesn't support it, and stick to it until it becomes a core belief.

Remember, every life level requires a different you. Think about that…EVERY LIFE LEVEL REQUIRES A DIFFERENT YOU. Just look at your own life. What are some examples of drastic changes you have attempted in your own life? Change requires that you change your perceptions.

Imagine a gopher that hides from hungry birds during the day. Most gophers will not leave their burrows during the day unless some emergency happens. For example, flooding the burrow gives the gopher the choice of *certain* death by drowning or *possible* death by escaping. In this example, the risk of following the normal routine becomes greater than the risk of doing something different.

Humans work the same way, except that our fears are based on past experiences combined with future anticipations. These fears are not real. They are imagined. They are a made-up story based on past experiences and programming that are designed to keep us safe. Just like the gopher, we weigh out the pain of staying where we are, not taking a risk, staying where we are comfortable, versus doing something in a different way that may be painful or uncomfortable.

Our routines form what's known as our comfort zone. We refer to doing things we don't normally do as "leaving the comfort zone." How did you feel the last time you left your comfort zone? Maybe someone asked you to deliver a short speech to a group of your peers. You may have felt scared, nervous, insecure, and ready to bolt at a moment's notice. This is a perfect example of our prey instincts telling us to get back in our comfort zone as quickly as possible.

I remember my first experience speaking. I literally thought I would be killed and eaten! I was to speak for 20 minutes to a group of about 20 people. I prepared for a month. I must have written 20 pages of notes. I couldn't stop thinking about it. What might happen if I didn't do it right, or forgot what I was supposed to say, or I might say it wrong, make a mistake—the list was endless.

I was staying in a hotel the night before I was to speak. I couldn't sleep, for fear of being killed and eaten! I tried to think of ways I could get out of speaking. Nothing seemed to make any sense. Then, I came up with the answer. I will have an accident on the way to the speaking engagement. Not a huge one. Just something small, but big enough that I could show my dented fender, so it looked legit. I figured the accident would be less painful than speaking.

Just as I went for the door to leave to stage my accident, someone knocked. I thought it was probably housekeeping, so I opened the door. It wasn't housekeeping. It was my associate that had booked the speaking engagement for me. He said, "I came to pick you up." My first thought was, *'You are going to be in an accident.'*

I said, "I'll drive."

He said, "No, I'll drive."

I said, "No, I want to drive."

He said, "I'm parked in front of the door. I'm driving."

I thought, *'Do I grab the wheel of his car and have an accident?'* I decided not to do that, but to follow through with the speech instead.

We arrived. My heart was pounding. I felt like I wanted to throw up. I was terrified. I took a few deep breaths and started my talk. I spoke for 20 minutes and I have no idea what I said. When I finished, I immediately went outside and stood beside the car and did a lot of deep breathing to regain my composure.

'Never again,' was what I was thinking. After a few moments, I thought, *'I have one of two choices: never do it again or do it often until I get better at it.'* After a lot of mental back and forth, I chose the latter.

I was in charge of about 300 salespeople that did presentations for small to medium sized groups to sell seminar tickets for a Jim Rohn seminar. I put the word out that I was available to do up to three presentations a day for groups of fifty or more…which I did for the next five years. And after about 15 presentations a week for a few years, I finally lost my fear of being killed and eaten by an audience. I created a new belief, a program that was stronger than the old one.

The stronger the urge to get back to your comfort zone, the farther you stray. This happens because our brains are wired to learn and follow habits designed to keep us safe and alive. We do this by learning how our predators behave, and then creating patterns to avoid them, even if our predators only exist in our imagination. Like the "no" that the salesperson gets over and over, until now they are afraid to even prospect. The "no" becomes the predator. Like the person that has been hurt multiple times in a relationship. And now the thought of getting involved in another relationship becomes very scary. Or the person who has made several attempts in business and loses money. The thought of losing money again is the predator.

The comfort zone is nothing more or less than behavioral boundaries set by your core beliefs that were either formed when you were too young to understand what was happening, or over a long period of time through repeated experiences.

Core beliefs form your entire reality from birth to death unless you take action to change them. The good news is that you can change your beliefs. We do it all the time. Just think of something you used to believe that you no longer believe. Do you still believe what you believed in high school? Once you got out into the real world, you most likely looked back and laughed at some of the stupid things you did and what you believed to be true once you realized it wasn't true at all.

It's like earning a six-figure income. Once you hit it, if that's the case, now you believe you can, so you settle for nothing less. That's called creating a new belief. The catch is that changing your beliefs will force you to confront programming that your brain interprets as being essential for your very survival.

Again, this is why crash diets, New Year's resolutions, joining a gym, opening a savings account, cutting up the credit cards, and other drastic changes rarely last more than a few days to a few weeks. At some point, the desire for change surrenders to the brain's built-in attempts to keep you from getting killed and eaten. Unless you decide and commit to experiencing the pain of change, and you stick with it until you change, nothing changes. What are some examples of drastic changes you have attempted in your own life? How have they worked out for you?

How can you change when you run up against instincts designed to keep you safe and alive? A prey animal needs to react to predators without question. And if you want change, you have to become self-observant to determine what you should act upon and what is old programming that no longer serves your greater good.

Indecision causes hesitation. And if you hesitate, you could get killed and eaten! Hesitation gives predators an extra split second to move in for the kill. So, you end up making a quick, irrational decision based on core beliefs that may not be true.

It's starts with a decision to change whatever it is you want to change. So, when one of those old programs arise, stop! Stop and ask yourself, *"If I proceed, will this take me in the direction I want to go? Is this fear real or in my imagination, based on old programming?"*

Take a good look at any animal whose parents raise the young. The young stick around to learn the survival skills they need. Prey animals learn when they can come out, where to go, how to avoid predators, and when to retreat back home. Their survival depends on absorbing this information and mastering the skills without question. We were taught similar things. "That's hot, don't touch that, you'll go blind. Careful, you'll fall."

Of course, certain things we have learned have become essential to our survival. But unlike prey animals, we humans are programming our young from birth until they leave home, good or bad, right or wrong. We are programmed about money based on how rich or poor our parents were and how they handled money. We were programmed about relationships, good or bad, based upon our parents' relationship. We were programmed regarding our eating habits, how we think, attitudes, and so on…good or bad.

Again, all beliefs are false, until you decide they are true. The dictionary defines belief as, "To hold an opinion." We are programmed and convinced that our beliefs are true, whether they are true or not. In other words, we see and experience our beliefs as true. Two plus two equals four because we believe it does. If you believe that two plus two equals five, then no amount of argument will convince you otherwise, unless you choose to change that belief.

Beliefs equal truth because they are the mental sunglasses that filter your senses before you perceive the sensation. Your reticular activating system selects which sensory input is important based on your beliefs. Change a belief, and your view of the world changes, as well as the view others have of you. Your beliefs color every bit of the input you receive. Only when you believe something do you become aware of the sensation of the input.

If your personal reality is based on core beliefs, then the universe that each of us experiences is not the cause but rather the effect of whatever is left over after our core beliefs do their work.

The statement, "I'll believe it when I see it," is backward. We actually see things *because* we believe them. This has some amazing implications when you start to look at life in this way.

Think about it. We see things *because* we believe it. Back to what I said earlier. When you change a belief, your view of the world changes.

So, what is the answer to changing? The answer, or rather the challenge, is to take the negative past out of the present. The real goal should be to have your present empty of the negative past and not to give the past meaning unless you say so.

Self-observation is the key.

Is what I'm giving energy to right now taking me where I want to go? Is this fear, feeling, emotion, or conflict supportive or non-supportive? Bottom line—is it true, or is it something you have been programmed to believe is true?

To change a belief, you have to challenge it.

Is it true?

What experience do you have that makes it true?

How do you know it to be true?

Who taught you to believe this?

What if they didn't know?

What if it's not true?

Who would you be without this belief?

What action should you take next?

When you achieve this level of control, you will experience what is known as true emotional freedom. You'll have the freedom to choose fascination over frustration, success over failure, calm over upset. When you take responsibility and observe reality—in other words, what's really happening—you can then choose to create whatever reality you want.

Start today, by identifying a story you have been telling yourself that has held you back in life. Example: I can't get ahead financially. That's a story, not reality. It is not true unless you say it is.

I can't seem to keep a relationship together…

It's hard to lose weight…

Pick a story, just one to start. Look for the truth, then take action based upon that truth. The question is, does your interpretation of this story serve you or hold you back? Notice what you say to yourself about what has happened, and then exercise the freedom to choose a different interpretation.

I don't want you to believe me. I want you to try it and experience the result for yourself. You'll experience a positive result the very first time you try.

WATCH OUT FOR THOSE PREDATORS!

Thirteen

Live in the Moment

"Many people think they are living in the moment, when in reality they are fearfully running from one moment to the next."

--- Jim Britt

While at work, do you find yourself thinking about how you are going to spend the weekend, then while trying to enjoy the weekend, your mind is on work?

Living in the moment means living in the present where all action takes place. And yet, we spend too much time living in the past or preparing for the future. Life doesn't happen yesterday, that's past. You can't earn more money or start a business in the past. It would be nice, however, to simply reach back into the past and erase the mistakes, press rewind, and make it all better, change the 'I wish I would have's' or erase the 'I should have's.' But that's not possible which makes it a waste of your time and energy. When living in the past you are actually reliving it. Wouldn't it be sad to get to the end of your life and realize that you lived only 10% of it because you were so busy living the past over and over again, like a rerun movie?

Life doesn't happen tomorrow either. It's not here yet. If you are continually waiting for real life to begin by convincing yourself that life will be better when you find the perfect opportunity, when you make more money, get married, or when you retire, you are missing the value of today.

Bottom line is your life will always be filled with challenges and problems and the sooner you admit this to yourself, the sooner you can get on with your life and be happy with what we have, in pursuit of what you want.

It's not easy to always live in the moment because we are often taken out of the moment with circumstances that happen. You should have to plan for tomorrow. You should have to plan for the meeting next week. But when you are planning, wouldn't it be more effective to be in the moment instead of being in a state of anxiety about the meeting next week? Then, of course, when you are in the meeting, be in the meeting instead of mentally somewhere else or worrying about how the meeting will turn out. In other words, wherever you are, be there!

I'm not saying that you shouldn't retain your memories of the past, because you should. Even though there are some things that should be forgotten. You just need to be aware that you sometimes relive those memories over and over again allowing them to dictate how you live life in the present.

Living in the present makes you a better parent, a better spouse, a more effective entrepreneur and money maker, a happier person over all, and a better communicator; because when you are in the moment, you are there mentally, physically, emotionally, and spiritually. You can't escape the moment, but you do have control over that which you bring into the moment.

Our lives are made up of days, and within each day there are 1440 tiny miracles called moments. A life well lived is lived moment to moment where we receive the deepest blessings of our lives. Our lives should be like an adventure, like unwrapping hidden treasure. When you carefully open each moment to see what unfolds, life will unfold the most extraordinary miracles, personally and financially.

I remember once when my wife and I were in Hawaii. I was there to speak at a convention, and she went with me for a few extra days of relaxation. She was seven months pregnant with our second son. We were on the beach catching a few rays, and she wanted to tan her back. Not a small feat for someone seven months pregnant, needing to lie on her stomach. I got the bright idea to just dig a hole in the sand and let her belly drop down below the surface. It turned out to be a humorous experience not only for us but for the people on the beach who were close enough to watch.

Later that afternoon at the tiki bar, I ran into the fellow that was next to us on the beach that got such a kick out my wife burying her belly in the sand. Turns out he was the head of a big company and was looking for a keynote speaker at three of his regional events. I invited him to sit in on my keynote the next day. Long story short, I got scheduled for all three of his events with a very nice fee for each.

Later that evening, my wife and I enjoyed the most remarkable sunset and had a delightful dinner at Hawaii's most romantic restaurant. I don't remember much of anything else about the trip, even the company I was speaking for, the hotel…nothing. But I vividly remember all three experiences and will for the rest of my life. Why? Because I was fully present, in the moment, as they were happening.

Look back at your own life. You don't remember everything that's ever happened, but you remember the experiences of moments. Like your first kiss, your first date, the first time you ate an artichoke, etc.

The key to finding and experiencing this moment and all its newness, again and again, is slowing down to the speed of life as it happens. Not the speed of light, but the speed of life. What's the hurry anyway? There's no prize for being the fastest human in the maze! What makes this and every moment so special is that it continually releases the freshness of living. Each moment is a new beginning. The more you slow down and experience the moments, the faster you will achieve the results you are looking for.

The next time you feel inconvenienced for any reason, traffic, lines, etc. see it as a signal to slow down, to enjoy your surroundings, to be present with your situation. When you are being delayed, you are being asked to open up and to take a look around. You may be surprised at what you see and experience. The next time you feel stuck or lost in anxiety, stop and start a new moment.

Matt, the main character (me) in my book Rings of Truth, while on the island of Kauai, backpacked into Kalalau Valley on the North Shore of Kauai. As he hiked the narrow trail, questions continually occupied his thoughts. "What should I be doing with my life? What is truth? What is real?" He was so self-absorbed he didn't even see the beauty around him. He missed the thousand-foot waterfalls and the rock archways. He was so absorbed in yesterday's problems and what he was going to do with his future, that he totally ignored the plants, the trees, and the beauty all around him.

After hiking for several hours, Matt stopped for a break at Hanakoa Valley, the half-way point on the trail. A little cabin, set back in the trees, offered a resting place for hikers. He took advantage of the opportunity and went inside. Another hiker, a woman by the name of Nan, coming from the opposite direction had decided to do the same. He introduced himself, and they quickly became friends. After a few hours of visiting, he told her of his concerns about his future. In her wisdom, she explained to him that he had to figure out his own answers to the questions harbored in his mind. Until then, he wasn't ready to know the answers. She went on to say that he had much to discover, that he should treat his discoveries a little more like a treasure hunt and a little less like the burden of his existence. She said that if he did, he would have a lot more fun and accomplish much more.

As they prepared to go different directions, she turned to Matt and said, "You might try not thinking so much, but rather feeling more. All the answers are in you already; you just need to get out of the way so they can come out. Remember to enjoy the journey! And also remember that life happens for you, not to you. Aloha."

I know the story of Matt very well, because he played "me" in my life story—Rings of Truth. Pick up a copy. I guarantee reading it will be the most life changing experience you will ever have.

We all experience fears in our lives that keep us bouncing back and forth between yesterday and tomorrow, but most fear we experience is imagined and protectively stored within our subconscious for later playback.

To live in the present makes it possible to let go of the feelings that keep the real you trapped inside. Begin to see and feel the wonders around you just as Matt was able to, once he let go of the fear that prevented him from living in the moment. He could now appreciate the rock archways and every tree and plant he touched and smelled as he passed them. When he began to live in the moment, he could actually feel the peace that existed on the island of Kauai and inside him. He was learning to feel instead of thinking all the time. And any one of us can do the same through applying this example in our own lives.

I'm not suggesting that you have to go to some exotic place to find yourself. What I am suggesting is that you just see the beauty of whatever is around you. It is not where you are, but how you perceive where you are that counts. Wherever you are, be there in every sense of the word. Life only happens right now, this moment. It doesn't happen any other time, so any time you are in the past or the future, you are out of life. Don't let life pass you by, whatever you do. Figure out for yourself what it is you need to know and treat the discovery a little more like a treasure hunt and a little less like the burden of your existence. You'll have a lot more fun and your entrepreneurial experience will flourish. Find what it is you are here to do, your wealth secret, your gift, then just relax and do it. Think less, feel more. The answers are already in you. You just need to get your mind out of the way, so they surface. This is not a small life for you. Remember to enjoy the journey.

In Hawaii, "Aloha" is a spiritual expression of love. The Aloha Spirit is the coordination of the heart and mind within each individual, bringing one back to oneself.

As you live in the moment, that is exactly what you are doing, coordinating the mind with the heart and bringing you back to yourself. True happiness is in the moment, success happens in the moment. All that is real is in the moment. To live each moment is a gift we give ourselves.

There are two quotes from the Bible I always remember. "And time shall be no more." This statement simply means, "One day we will all live in the present." Only our subconscious programs cause you to speculate about what will happen tomorrow or relive what happened yesterday.

Another of my favorite quotes from the Bible is, "Many are called, but few are chosen." In other words, "Few listen." To live each moment is a gift we give ourselves. Once we have achieved that, then realize your gift to listen. I'm not talking about listening with your ears. I'm talking about listening with your heart. The gift of listening with your heart gives you the power to smooth the rough edges of your human imperfections. When you listen with your heart, your intuition, you see reality as it is. When you listen with your mind, we most often try to mold reality into what we think it should be instead of what it is.

When you look back at your life, most of your moments remembered are usually acts of almost breathtaking simplicity. They happen to each of us every day, and many times during the day. It could be something as simple as giving someone you love a single rose, a sip of fine wine, soaking in a beautiful sunset, a kind word, a smile, a hug, sharing a meal with your family, or someone special to you. Or it could be a contact or opportunity showing up at exactly the right time. Any of these performed in the moment with mind-fullness will nourish the soul and give your life true meaning.

The ordinary riches of human life are made up of the moments that you truly live within. So, take your time, savor each and every moment. And above all, be open to being surprised. Life is full of miracles, but miracles only happen in the moment to those who are open to receive. Awaken to the freshness of each moment as it greets you.

FOR ONE DAY, EVERY TIME YOU FEEL YOUR MIND DRIFTING BACK IN THE PAST OR FORWARD INTO THE FUTURE, CONSCIOUSLY BRING YOUR ATTENTION BACK TO THE PRESENT. TRY IT FOR ONE WEEK AND NOTICE HOW MUCH MORE EFFECTIVE YOU ARE IN ALL AREAS OF YOUR LIFE.

Fourteen

There is Power in Letting Go

"Letting go is not the anxious search for new solutions to old problems. It's creating space for new solutions to come to you."

--- Jim Britt

Imagine walking into a room where groups of people are seated at a table, a succulent meal set before them. Their table is filled with every sort of food you can imagine. It's a mouth-watering display, all perfectly prepared. It's all right in front of their noses, easily within their reach.

You notice however, that none of these people are eating. They haven't taken a single bite. Their plates are empty, and it appears that they have been seated there for a very long time, so long that they appear to be starving to death.

They are starving, not because they cannot see or eat all the food before them, or because eating is forbidden or harmful; they are not eating because they don't realize that food is what they need. They don't know that those very sharp pains in their stomachs are caused by hunger. They don't see that all they need to do to stop their suffering is eat the food that's right in front of them.

This is an example of our basic human suffering as well. Most of us sense that there is something wrong, that something is inherently missing in our lives, but we haven't a clue how to overcome the problem. We may have an inkling that what we need is somehow very close to us, but we don't connect the lack of it to the sharp pain inside us. With time, as the pain becomes even more severe, we start to believe that being in pain is just a normal part of living.

Many years ago, I kept noticing that so many people feel stuck. As hard as they tried to break free, they kept ending up in the same place over and over again. Sort of like an exciting ride on a roller coaster that drops you off at the same place you started.

A woman in one of my workshops shared that the reason she couldn't become financially successful was because of the way her dad treated her growing up.

She said, "My dad verbally abused me. He repeatedly told me that I would never amount to anything, that I would never be successful at anything, and that I would never be as good as my brother and sister."

To confirm, I asked, "So the reason you can never be successful is because of your dad and how he abused you verbally?"

She answered, "Yes."

I then asked, "Where is your dad now?"

She said, "He died ten years ago."

I then asked, "If your dad died ten years ago, who is abusing you now?"

She said, "I don't understand the question."

I asked again, "Well, if your dad is no longer around, who is abusing you now?"

Looking a bit puzzled, she came back with, "I still don't understand the question."

I said, "You think about it for a while, and I'll be back in a few minutes." I continued with the workshop. I would occasionally glance in her direction, and she looked very deep in thought. After about twenty-minutes I asked her, "Well, did you come up with the answer to my question?"

Still looking puzzled, she said, "No."

I said, "You keep thinking about it, and I'll be back in a bit."

After asking her the same question two more times, she responded with, "You mean, I'm abusing myself?"

"What do you think?" I asked.

She responded with, "I don't know."

A few minutes later, I returned and asked, "Well, did you come up with the answer?"

Her response was, "Oh my God, I have been abusing myself for the last ten years! Is that what you meant by how we get programmed? Is that a core belief of mine that is holding me back?"

"Yup, you guessed it," I said.

I worked with her for another ten minutes to help her clear that program, which she did. Last I heard, she was doing well financially.

That's an example of how our mental programming can keep us stuck, repeating the same addictive cycle over and over again.

Let's say you are feeling the pain of not having enough money. You suffer from it daily, unaware that you can eliminate your suffering and start to earn more by simply making the right choices and letting go of those habit patterns holding you back. The problem is that our emotional conflicts are so familiar to us that they keep us blinded to better possibilities. We actually become addicted to feeling the way we do, thinking that it is 'just the way things are' and we resign ourselves to just getting by and coping.

The million-dollar question for a lot of people is, "How do we let go and walk away from what's familiar to us? How do we let go of our pain and conflicts?" I believe that most people have a desire to do more with their lives, to be happy, to be financially successful, and not suffer their emotional pains. However, most often their fear of taking risks and the pain of change prevents them from even trying. We very often fear what we want most. And at the same time, we get what we fear most. Our mental programming is so averse to risk that it prefers to keep us safe and secure within the status quo, so we stay where we are even though we are miserable. Just look around you. You see it everywhere. If most people want to be happy and successful financially, what is it that keeps them from making the changes they need to make to get there? People say they want to change, but do they really? Better yet, are they willing to look inside and confront the real issues that are holding them back?

Do a little exercise. Do you feel that you are more successful now than five years ago? Have you truly made significant progress? Have the last five years turned out the way you wanted them to be? And if not, why not? What's stopping you from making the changes you want? I'm guessing that you already know what it is that needs changing.

When you break free from the patterns of the past and begin to see the truth behind the conflict watch what happens to your life. People, experiences, and opportunities will begin to flow to you. You'll begin to see conflict as just a mental and emotional mistake. Letting go of conflict is a choice. When faced with a conflict, ask yourself this very important question. "What benefit am I getting from holding on to this conflict? Does it serve my higher good? Am I willing to trade an abundant life for hanging onto something that doesn't serve my higher good? Am I willing to spend my vital energy on something that doesn't take me in the direction I want to go?"

Many experts say just face your fears, do the thing you fear most and the fear will go away. Well, that's easy to say, and even makes sense when you hear it, but how about all the people who are afraid to face their fears, too afraid to take the first step? What do they do? What about that buried feeling attached to the fear, what happens to that?

Let's face it. Life is risky. Going into business is risky. Getting married is risky. Snow skiing, mountain climbing, driving past the speed limit, raising children are all risky. I could go on and on. All these activities are risky, but we choose to do them anyway, don't we?

Let's first gain an understanding of the true definition of fear. Fear is taking a past experience, projecting it into the future, with the anticipation of it happening again, and then re-living it in the moment. Fear is simply trapped energy you hold inside that was created from a past traumatic experience, or series of experiences over time. Fear is a mental mistake. It's a made-up story. It's friction in your thought process. When you get hurt emotionally, you feel the pain inside. Then, you hold onto that painful experience hoping that it will protect you from it happening again, but it won't. Fear is simply trapped energy wanting to be released. And once you gain that understanding, it becomes easier to let it go of the fear.

Look at it this way. Every action you take is either based in fear or love. If you move toward what you love, you naturally move away from what you fear. While you are moving toward what you love, feel the fear, face it yes, but do more than that. Observe it. Separate yourself from it and see it for what it is, which is just a made-up story, a mental mistake. It's your subconscious programming bringing it up saying, "Hey, do you need this anymore or would you like to delete it?" Your fear is NOT you. It's just a passenger you have picked up along the way. It is not hanging onto you, instead you are hanging on to it! You are the CEO of your thoughts, feelings, and emotions.

When a fear feeling surfaces, breathe into it, and when you exhale, let it go. Then, take a course of action that will bring you more of what you love. Just the fact that you have observed yourself feeling the fear, and you see it for what it really is, you have weakened its hold on you, or rather your hold on it.

Letting go is a choice, moment to moment. It's a fork in the road. It's a choice to buy into the delusion of our mind chatter, of past pains and programming, or move toward what you would love to have in your life.

If you want to increase your level of productivity, once you have decided what you want to accomplish, ask yourself moment to moment, "Is this action moving me toward my desired outcome or further away." Success at anything is that simple.

Whatever happened to you in the past is not happening to you now, unless you allow it to. The past is only your story, and it's not real today. It's a memory, a trapped energy pattern. It's like an old movie that you keep watching over and over, until you decide you've watched it enough.

What's real is the stress, headache, anxiety, the lack of success, and unhappiness you've created for yourself out of something that doesn't exist any longer. That's what's real. Think about it.

Any sort of permanent change, whether it be losing weight, quitting smoking, getting healthier, earning more money, having a more fulfilling relationship, or breaking an emotional addictive cycle, requires several things.

If you want to break an addictive cycle, the first thing required is a desire to break it. You have to want something bad enough in order to make any permanent change. Desire has to come from inside you. No one else can create that for you. I'm assuming that you have a desire to change, otherwise you wouldn't be reading this book.

The next step is that you must make a decision to change. A decision to do one thing eliminates something else. For example, if you want to be wealthy, you have to first make a decision to "be" a wealthy person. Once that decision is made, it eliminates the decision to do anything less. You can't have the mindset of a wealthy person and one that can't pay his bills every month simultaneously. You have to honor one and let go of the other. You can't make both decisions at the same time. You might say, "Well, I am working on developing a wealth mindset." If that's the case, you have chosen to be the person that can't pay his bills monthly. You are one or the other—fat or skinny, healthy or non-healthy, wealthy or not, drug user or not. Whatever it is you want, it is not a decision to "give it a try," but a decision to do it!

When you take steps to change, you'll always be faced with discomfort, fears, and doubt. In fact, changing can bring up your deepest fears—fears of failing… "What if I can't do this? What if it doesn't work? What will others think of me if I fail? I tried before and failed. What if I can't do it this time?" The list goes on and on. It can even bring up the fear of success— "What if I'm successful? Will I have to change? Can I handle the change? Will I be okay without my excuses? And trust me, suffering, misery, and conflict are all excuses, crutches, that you'll remain attached to for life until you decide to let them go and do something in a different way than you've done in the past. Change requires that you change. It's a battle between the old you and the new you.

Next, you have to stand by your decision and not let the mind chatter pull you down. Change can be like free falling out of an airplane;

it's both exhilarating and scary. You have to be so determined that you will let nothing throw you off course.

Whatever you're feeling, depression, anger, fear or anxiety, remember as it comes up, that it is just energy wanting to be released and that you are in complete control. As you feel it, stop for a moment and observe your feelings, then ask yourself these questions:

"Do I like feeling this way?" If your answer is "no," move on to the next question.

"Will honoring this feeling take me in the direction I want to go?" If your answer is "no," move on to the next question.

"Do I want to let it go?" If your answer is "yes," move on to the next question.

"Am I willing to let it go?" If your answer is "yes," then move to the last question.

"When...when will I let it go?"

And your answer should be apparent...NOW!

By the time you get to the last question, you'll discover that the feeling has left you. It may come back, but you have advanced to the next level. With each release, the feelings get weaker and less frequent.

Hanging on to your excuses requires a tremendous amount of energy, sometimes all your energy, and it will get you nowhere except backwards to more of the same. Letting go, on the other hand, requires no energy at all. It's simply a choice!

The most important thing is to love yourself above all. Then, fall in love with what you want to accomplish in life. The only other option is to fall in fear with it.

Any feeling that is not loving toward yourself, or what you want to accomplish, is based in fear. Darkness is the absence of light, just like fear is the "feeling" of the absence of love.

One of the most basic fears we have about letting go is the fear of the emptiness we believe will be there when we do. But in reality, when you die to the old, a vacuum is created for the new.

That empty space is instantly filled with passion, new ideas, and opportunities. When you simply surrender a fear, the vacuum is filled with what you need to fulfill your dreams and ambitions. If you are looking to find the next step to move forward, but are experiencing the fear of failing, there is no space for the new idea to come into view.

If you become an observer of your emotions—really observe them—you will no longer be attached to them or controlled by them. You can just allow them to "be there" without acting on them. With practice, you will eventually come to the realization that the origin of suffering can be put aside and let go of.

Letting go simply means that you leave emotions as they are. Whatever you pay attention to grows in strength. What you don't pay attention to withers away from lack of attention. It does not mean that they are gone forever, even though some will be. It is observing and letting them be. Through the practice of letting go you'll begin to realize that hanging on to outdated experiences, feelings, and emotions is the origin of suffering and conflict. You'll realize that all conflict is self-conflict.

When you find yourself attached to a feeling or emotion, look at it this way. If you are holding onto this book and you set it down on the table, you have let it go. Just because you have the book in your hand doesn't mean you have to carry it with you day after day for the rest of your life. The book is not the problem, just like the emotional suffering is not the problem. The problem is hanging on to it. So, what do you do? Let it go, lay it aside. You simply put it down, gently without any kind of conflict, just like putting the book on the table and walking away.

Now, this doesn't mean you don't handle problems that arise. Handle your problems, yes, but do it without the emotional attachment.

You can apply this insight to letting go of fear, anger, anxiety, disappointment, depression, or any other self-conflict. So, when you are feeling inner conflict, the moment that you refuse to indulge in that feeling, you are letting go, and you are in control.

We all have moments when everything we do just seems to work. It is during these times that great insights occur. We feel abundant, happy, and trusting of life. We are refreshingly still inside, our usual nagging "chatter" is quiet, and our energy flow is profoundly open. In this state we are able to experience our own true nature, love, passion, productivity, and the full beauty of our surroundings. We feel alive, balanced, and purposeful. Then suddenly, without any notice at all, this vibrant, loving state disappears as mysteriously as it came. Our soaring spirit seems to fall back to sleep, as we drift back into our old identity. We begin to once again "buy into" the illusionary, self-created tensions of worry, fear, depression, anxiety and scarcity, which restrict us from being in the moment and living the life we want. It's an up and down cycle, but the more you practice letting go, the easier it gets and the more peaceful and productive you become.

Remember that any feeling that is not taking you where you want to go is based in fear. When you let go of fear, all you have left is that empty space that can be filled with the answers you seek. Letting go leaves you with that feeling you had when you first fell in love. Love is an energy that travels so fast that it's everywhere at once. Even in your darkest moments, love is always present when you let go of what you fear. In fact, it is love presenting you with the fear saying, *'If you let go of this, you can have more of me.'*

We have some misconceptions about love, however. The first is that it comes from outside us, and the second is that it is secured through relationships. If we narrow love down to these two things, we are cheating ourselves out of the endless possibilities that exist. Love is always present inside us. It's just that we've disconnected by buying into our fears.

The depth of connection you feel becomes stronger as you let go of the fear, doubt, anger, blame, etc. Love is the spirit that lives within each of us. It's where all things originate.

Let me explain. Many years ago, a friend asked me what I thought the word resourceful meant? I said, maybe a few things, "Being productive. Using your imagination. Using your time wisely."

Later, I started thinking about the word resourceful. Could not get it off my mind. I looked up the definition and Webster defined it… RE-SOURCE-FUL. "Once again full of source." I thought that was interesting. Then, I looked up the key word "source," and it was defined as, "Where all things originate." It didn't say, some things, but _all_ things.

I spent the next two years trying to find another definition for "source." I looked on the internet, but it was pretty new, so not much there. Every time I was in a bookstore, I would search for it in the origin of words books. Then, I was presenting a 13-city seminar tour in the UK and one of the stops was a small village, called Chester. While out walking one afternoon, I saw a sign on the back door of an antique bookstore. Intrigued, I went in the back door. Immediately, I saw an old dictionary about eight inches thick. It looked to be really old. It had a sign on it: Do not open. Do not touch. I thought that probably meant for local residents and surely not me. (smile) I carefully opened the book and looked up the word "source." I found multiple definitions that I had seen before, but one simple one jumped off the page at me. Source, defined as, *"Love."*

Re-source-ful: *"Once again full of love."* As I said before we have two choices, to operate out of fear or love. Example, when you decide to accomplish something you fall, *"in love"* with it. And if you let mind chatter, circumstances, or other people's opinion influence you to lose site of what you want, you fall *"in fear"* with it. And when you are presented with a fear, it is love, *"where ALL things originate,"* presenting you with the fear, saying "if you let go of this fear, you can have more of what you'd love."

Once you begin the process of letting go, you see that every seemingly painful event is truly a gift designed to show us the power of love, if we'll just let go and embrace it. Remember, what you pursue will always elude you. What you become is what you'll create. If you pursue love, it will always be "out there" somewhere, in the next relationship, job, success, money, or outside event. When you love yourself, you'll begin to discover love in everything you do, and in everyone you meet.

Receiving comes first, then giving. And what you give to others, you also give to yourself in return. But, you have to be open to receiving before you have anything to give. And of course, the reverse is also true: What you withhold from yourself, you withhold from others, and again from yourself.

Letting go is essential in living a personal or financially successful life.

WHEN YOU ARE "IN LOVE," ENERGY FLOWS AS IT SHOULD, AND SO DOES YOUR SUCCESS AND HAPPINESS.

Fifteen

Energy Gainers and Drainers

"We don't accomplish great things because we engage in things not so great."

--- Jim Britt

There's nothing worse, when you want to get things done, than to be too tired to think and perform efficiently. Peak performance requires a high level of energy. And high energy requires a total commitment to being fit and healthy. By putting more energy into what you do, you will automatically get more results, in less time.

Most people spend their younger years trying to accumulate wealth, then later in life they spend their wealth trying to regain their health! The sad truth is that most people take better care of their car than they do their bodies. They feed their dog better than they do themselves! They maintain their homes better than they maintain their health!

It's really amazing to me what some people put into their bodies on a regular basis, and then complain that they get sick or are too tired to perform the way they want.

I made a decision about forty years ago that I was going to be a healthy person. I decided that taking care of my health was going to be a priority for me from that point forward. When I ask people, "What is the most important thing to you in life?" Most people's answer is health and family. However, when you look at where most people spend 75% of their waking hours, it's chasing money, whether in a job or their own business. Then, when you ask what they do to take care of their health (exercise, eat right, etc.), the answer usually goes something like this: "Well, after working long hours, I really don't have time to exercise, and I sort of eat on the run."

Then, when they get home there's little or no time with the family. In my opinion, when it really comes down to being more productive and feeling good, being healthy should always be at the top of the list, no matter what. At least it should be. The problem is that most people put it at the bottom of their list until they get sick. Then it goes to the top of the list!

Keep this in mind. When it comes to health, you will always endure one of two pains in life: the pain of discipline or the pain of regret. The pain of discipline weighs ounces while the pain of regret can weigh tons! The discipline it takes to stay healthy and keep your energy at its optimum will reap tremendous rewards—and they will be immediate! You'll feel better, think more clearly, have more energy, be more productive, and get more done in less time. It's like the Fram oil filter company's slogan, *"Pay me now or pay me later."* Pay up front for an oil filter to keep your oil clean or pay for an engine overhaul later. Take care of your health now or pay with sickness later.

I'm not a trained nutritionist, but I do know a lot about how to stay healthy. To me, the body is pretty simple. Its natural state is health. Let me put it another way. Your health is a gift and disease is something you earn. Health is natural. Disease is something you give yourself! You don't "catch" a disease. Whether it is cancer, a headache, the flu, or anything else, you give it to yourself through a lack of doing the necessary things to stay healthy.

If you experience ongoing fatigue, midday energy slumps, headaches, irritability if you miss a meal, cloudy thinking, memory recall problems, or crave the intake of stimulants like Coke, coffee, sugar, cigarettes, etc., then you probably suffer from a nutritional deficiency of some sort—one that you gave to yourself. Want to increase your productivity by 10% or more? Stop it!

In order to gain a high level of performance, you must rid yourself of *energy drainers,* and replace them with *energy gainers,* like live nutritionally rich food and a daily exercise program of some sort.

Drinking a cup of coffee is an energy drainer. It may feel at the time like an energy gainer, but there's a let-down coming. And anyone who drinks coffee knows what I'm talking about.

Taking a short walk during the day is an energy gainer.

Eating refined foods like breakfast cereal is an energy drainer.

Eating fresh fruits is an energy gainer.

Eating fast foods for lunch or a heavy meal is an energy drainer.

Eating a nice sized salad for lunch is an energy gainer.

Alcohol for lunch is an energy drainer.

Fresh squeezed juice is an energy gainer.

Drinking sodas are an energy drainer.

If you want to operate at peak performance, you must ruthlessly eliminate anything that drains your energy and replace it with something that gains you energy.

Your body is constantly burning nutrients. If these are not replenished regularly, then the cells within your body begin to slow and die. The result is a slower thinking process, lack of energy, the inability to function efficiently, and eventually it leads to degeneration and disease, one that you've given to yourself. Most people are actually digging their grave with their teeth!

Most have grown to accept low energy as just a normal part of life—eat poorly, low energy, get tired, and perform poorly. When in fact, it is not normal at all, but it is common.

In order to accomplish uncommon goals, it requires being an uncommon person. And to do that requires having an uncommon level of energy and vitality.

Just remember, if your body fails you for an hour, a day, or longer, you're out of the game for that period of time. Peak performance requires a commitment to renewing your energy on a continuous basis. And if you are not aware of how much energy you are *draining,* and what's causing the drainage, or how much you are *gaining,* and what you are doing to gain it, chances are you'll run out of energy long before your 600 productive minutes run out each day.

I asked comedian George Burns once, at 97 years of age, if he had a secret to living as long as he had. He said, "Yes I do have a secret, and here it is. *Don't die!"* Then he said, "All kidding aside, your body is where you live, and you have to take care of it if you want to live a long, healthy life."

THE SIMPLE TRUTH OF THE MATTER IS THERE ARE NO DEAD PEAK PERFORMERS, ARE THERE?

Sixteen

Reinvent Your Money Philosophy

"The limit of your capacity to create is not determined by the limit of your current view."

--- Jim Britt

Once again, that uncomfortable feeling pays a visit, but this time you can't close the door and just ignore it. The discomfort that you are feeling is with yourself. You feel like your life does not fit you anymore, and maybe it hasn't for a long time. But, do you dare reinvent yourself and your money philosophy? Do you have the courage to take the necessary steps to let go of the person you are today, and used to be, so that you can blossom into the person you have always wanted to become financially?

This can sometimes feel scary because you have to let go of the attachments you currently have about money in order to reinvent your new money philosophy. If you are up to reinventing yourself, and ready to travel along a new path to where you have never been, now is the perfect time to get started, and I want to help.

The process of reinventing yourself is very empowering. In fact, you can apply this lesson to any area of your life. If you want something more in any area of life, you have to reinvent yourself into someone different than you are today. But this message is about reinventing your money philosophy.

You might not realize it yet, but you do have all it takes to truly ignite change financially. Don't let anybody else tell you otherwise. The skill of making money as an entrepreneur can be learned.

The first thing you need to do is take a look at yourself. What do you want to change about yourself? Because all change starts inside you. Since you are starting over so to speak, if you are going to dream, might as well dream big. Think of yourself as an author who is writing your new life story, your new money philosophy, and you are limited only by your imagination.

Before you start reinventing yourself, you have to at least know what you're working with and what you want changed. The more specific you are, the better. This will give you direction and allow you to focus on the right things to make the changes necessary.

As I said in the prior chapter…if you ask someone what the most important thing in their life is, most often they will answer family or their health. But is that actually true? Because, when you look at where the average person spends most of their waking hours, it is focused on making money. So money must be the most important area for most—at least until they have all they want to feel financially secure. Again, since you are reinventing yourself and your money philosophy, if you are going to dream, you might as well dream big.

I recently spoke with a man who shared with me that he had not been able to pay his bills fully or on time each month for twenty-five years! I asked him what he thought he needed to do to make a change.

He said, "Well, I have been thinking about cutting my overhead."

I said, "Well, there is nothing wrong with cutting your overhead, but in 60 to 90 days you'll be right back in the same situation."

He said, "Why would you say that?"

I said, "Because you are addicted to that way of life, and until something major happens that causes you to look inside for the answers, or someone like me guides you through the process of breaking that addiction, you'll live the rest of your life with it."

He said, "I have tried so many times to make more than I spend, but I can never make it happen. I've tried many different businesses, money making opportunities, but I always end up back in the same place financially."

Let me explain. We all have habit patterns that become second nature, both positive and negative ones. On the positive side, it would be hard to live without them. Walking for example. What if every time you stood up to walk across the room, you had to relearn to walk? It would make life a little tough. Or every time you got into your car, you had to relearn to drive. We do a lot of things second nature, like driving a car, skiing, swimming, walking, talking, riding a bike, etc.

What about the negative side? Consider all the mental programs that have shaped our lives in some way and have become second nature, like the man that could never pay his bills on time.

You see, we all have programs that have influenced our lives negatively. Let's say you want to be a financially successful entrepreneur, what can happen on the negative side is you are stuck in the "box" where the negative program, "money is hard to earn" lives. And the more you try to break free of the programming and fail, the stronger it becomes. To become wealthy, you have to look inside first and make changes, not outside.

One of the things I discovered in my career is that wealthy people think differently, and they do things that the majority of people are not willing to do. Most have been conditioned to believe that creating wealth is difficult, or that it's only for the lucky few.

You *can* have all the money you want. It just takes learning and developing the traits that rich people use, and some time to make it happen. If you want to change your financial situation, you have to reinvent yourself, because the old you won't cut it.

To become wealthy, you will have to learn the number sequence to the vault.

First, we already discussed, is a firm decision to become wealthy. Wealthy people you'll find make solid decisions and commit to seeing them through. Decision always comes before the answer. Poor people look for ways to become wealthy and never find it. Great opportunities are not within their view because they never make the decision to become wealthy.

Those who are not financially successful put off decisions or mess around with their decision once it is made, and then have a lot of excuses about why things aren't working. Mediocrity cannot be an option if you want to attain wealth; and wealth is whatever you say it is. A decision to be wealthy creates a wealth mindset, and your mindset determines how you show up in the world. It also determines how the world shows up to support you.

It's really surprising though how many people fear making that decision. They do all sorts of things to keep the moment of decision at arms-length including:

Gathering more data.

Getting ready to get going…

As soon as this or that happens, I'll get going…

I need to do more research.

Getting other's opinions.

Fretting over who the decision might offend.

Worrying about the resources needed to pull off the decision.

I'm hoping I'll just get lucky and make the money I need without making a decision, etc.

The real problem is that most are stuck in their comfort zone, and making a decision would mean having to do something different, something that might be a bit painful. I suppose that's a decision we all face—the pain of staying stuck in our current situation or the pain of change.

Most people would rather live with the "old you" for fear that becoming the "new you" would require too much pain.

If that's you, then you can stop reading now, and get back to the TV and potato chips. Because, if you are not willing to make a decision to change, no one can help you.

Your decision becomes an excuse, pointing the finger outwardly to some circumstance, etc.

I remember a friend of mine had created a hair care line to go into drugstore chains. He had the connections to get it into hundreds of stores across the country. However, after months, the line just wasn't selling. Instead of giving up, a business associate convinced him that he should try selling it on TV.

This was one of the first, if not the first, TV infomercial ever produced. So, nobody knew if it would actually work. My friend was a decision maker and a doer, so he said let's try it. That decision turned into over $200 million in sales that netted him roughly $70 to $100 million. The point is, he could have given up with his first attempt. One of the mega millionaires I interviewed filed bankruptcy three times and today has a net worth of over $500 million.

Don't give up just because one approach to becoming wealthy didn't work. There are thousands of ways to become wealthy, but without a wealth mindset, a decision to be wealthy, NOTHING…EVER… HAPPENS.

Seventeen

Think Like Superman

*"Waking up to your true greatness in life requires letting go of
who you imagine yourself to be."*

--- Jim Britt

FACT: Becoming a millionaire is easier than it has ever been.

Many people have the notion that it's an impossible task to become a millionaire. Some say, "It's pure luck." Others say, "You have to be born into a rich family." For others, "You'll have to win the Lotto." And for many they say, "Your parents have to help you out a lot." That's the language of the poor.

A single mother with five children says, "I want to believe in what you're saying. However, I'm 45 years old and work long hours at two dead-end jobs. I barely earn enough to get by. What should I do?"

Another man said, "Well, if you work for the government, you cannot expect to become a millionaire. After all, you're on a fixed salary and there's little time for anything else. By the time you get home, you've got to play with the kids, eat dinner, and fall asleep watching TV."

Everyone has a story as to why they could never become a millionaire. But for every story, excuse really, there are other stories OR PEOPLE with worse circumstances, that have become rich.

The truth is that all of us can become as wealthy as we decide to be. None of us is excluded from wealth. If you have the desire to receive money, whatever the amount, you have all of the rights to do so like everyone else. There's no limit to how much you can earn for yourself. The only limitations are what you place on yourself.

Money is like the sun. It does not discriminate. It doesn't say, "I will not give light and warmth to this flower, tree, or person because I don't like them." Like the sun, money is abundantly available to all of us who truly believe that it is for us. No one is excluded.

There are, however, some major differences between rich and poor people. Here are some tips for becoming rich.

Change Your Thinking

You have to see the bigger picture. There are opportunities everywhere! The problem is that most people see just trees, when they should be looking at the entire forest. By doing so you will see that there are opportunities everywhere. The possibilities are endless.

You'll also have to go through plenty of self-discovery before you earn your first million. Knowing the truth about yourself isn't always the easiest task. Sometimes, you'll find that you are your biggest enemy—at least some days.

Learn from Millionaires

Most people are surrounded by what I like to call their, "default friends." These friends are acquaintances that we see at the gym, school, work, local happy hour, and other places. We naturally befriend these people because we are all in the same boat financially. However, in most cases, these people aren't millionaires and cannot help you become one either. In fact, if you tell them you are going to become a millionaire, some may even tell you that it's impossible and discourage you from even trying. They'll tell you that you're living in a fantasy world and why you'll never be able to make it happen. Instead, learn from millionaires. Let go of these relationships that pull you down when it comes to your money desires. It's okay to have friends that aren't millionaires. However, only take input from those that have accomplished what you want to accomplish. Hang out with those that will encourage and help you get to the next level. Don't give your raw diamonds to a brick layer to be cut.

Indulge in Wealth

To become wealthy, you must learn about wealth. This means that you'll have to put yourself in situations that you've never been in before.

ON OCCASION, DO SOME OF THESE:

Fly first class and see how it makes you feel.

Eat out at the finest restaurant and don't look at the price.

Take a limo instead of a cab or Uber. Watch how you feel.

Reserve a suite in a first-class hotel.

If you are used to drinking a $20 bottle of wine, go for the $100 and see how it tastes. It does taste different.

All I am saying is, try some of the things that wealthy people do and see how it makes you feel.

Believe It's Possible

If you believe that it's possible to become a millionaire, you can make it happen. However, if you've excluded yourself from this possibility and think and believe that it's for other people, you'll never become a millionaire.

Also, be sure to bless rich people when you can. Haters of money aren't likely to receive any of it either.

Read books that have been written by millionaires. By gaining a well-rounded education about earning large sums of money and staying inspired, you'll be able to learn the wealth secrets of the rich. I just saw a video on LinkedIn with my friend Kevin Harrington from the TV show Shark Tank. He said that one of his new companies just had a million-dollar day on Amazon.

Enlarge Your Service

Your material wealth is the sum of your total contribution to society. Your daily mantra should be, *'How do I deliver more value to more people in less time?'* Then, you'll know that you can always increase your quality and quantity of service. Enlarging your service is also about going the extra mile. When it comes to helping others, you must give it everything you have. You just plant the seeds and nature will take care of the rest.

Seize ALL Opportunities That Make Sense

You cannot say "No" to opportunities and expect to become a millionaire. You must seize every opportunity that has your name on it. It may just be an opportunity to connect with an influential person for no reason. Sometimes the monetary reward will not come immediately, but if you keep planting seeds, eventually you'll grow a fruitful crop. Money is the harvest of the service you provide and sometimes the connections you have. The more seeds you plant, the greater the harvest.

Be Unstoppable

Want to know some of what my first mentor shared with me that took me from a broke factory worker, high school dropout, to millionaire?

First, he said, you have to start thinking like a wealthy, unstoppable person. He said that wealthy people think differently. He said, "I want you to start thinking like Superman!" Sounds crazy, right? Well it's not. It's powerful and here's why. How you think will change your life.

Wealthy people think differently. They really do. And anyone can learn to think like the wealthy.

I'm not talking about positive thinking, Law of Attraction, or motivation. Let's get real. None of that stuff works anyway. Otherwise we would all be rich and happy already. I'm talking about thinking based in quantum physics science. Once you understand and apply it, it will change your life. You will become unstoppable!

If there was any person, fictional or real, whose qualities you could instantly possess, who would that person be? Think about it. Personally, I would say that Superman is the perfect person. Now, you are probably thinking I have lost it right? Just stick with me here. I think you will like what you are about to hear.

Superman is a fictional superhero widely considered to be one of the most famous and popular action hero and an American cultural icon.

I remember watching Superman every Saturday morning when I was a kid. I couldn't get enough. He was my hero!

Let's look at Superman's traits:

Superman is indestructible.

He's a man of steel.

He can stop a locomotive in its tracks.

Bullets bounce off him.

He's faster than a speeding bullet.

No one can bring him down.

He can leap tall buildings in a single bound. Great powers to have in this day-and-age, wouldn't you say? What else would you need?

Now, for all you females, don't worry, we have not left you out. There is also a female version of Superman, named Superwoman. She has the same powers as Superman.

Now, this is where it gets interesting. Let's first look at the qualities that Superman possesses that you want to make your own. And to make it simple, I will refer to Superman for the rest of this message, and you can replace with Superwoman if you are female.

Again:

Superman is powerful and fearless.

Superman is virtually indestructible—except for kryptonite of course.

Superman can stop bullets.

Superman has supernatural powers. He can see through walls.

Superman can stop a speeding locomotive.

Superman can stop a bullet.

Superman jumps into immediate action when troubles arise.

Superman can crash through barriers.

Superman can even change clothes in a phone booth in seconds. Not too many of those around anymore. You'll have to duck behind a building to change.

So, you're thinking right now, *'Ok, I know that Superman has incredible supernatural powers, how can that help me? What good will it do me to think I am Superman, a fictional character?'*

Here is where science comes in. This is the part where you will be amazed when you learn about the supernatural powers that you already possess! NO, REALLY!

Your brain makes certain chemicals called neuro peptides. These are literally the molecules of emotion, like love, fear, joy, passion, and so on. These molecules of emotion are not only contained in your brain, they actually circulate throughout your cellular structure. They send out a signal, a frequency much like a radio station sending out a signal. For example, you tune to 92.5 and you get jazz. Tune to 99.6 and you get rock. And if you are just one decimal off, you get static. The difference is that your signal goes both ways. You are a sender and a receiver.

You put out a signal of confidence about your financial success and people, circumstances, and opportunities show up to support your success. When you put out a signal of doubt and uncertainty and you receive support for your doubt and uncertainty. You've been around someone that you didn't trust, or you felt less than positive just being in their presence, right? You have also been around people that inspire you. That's what I'm talking about. You are projecting a frequency, looking to resonate with the frequency you are transmitting.

Anyway, the amazing part about these cells of emotion is that they are intelligent. They are thinking cells. These cells are constantly eavesdropping on the conversation that you are having with yourself. That's right. They are listening to you! And others are listening to your cells as well. Others feel what you feel when they are around you.

Your unconscious mind, your cells, are listening in, waiting to adjust your behavior based on what they hear from you, their master. So just imagine what would happen if you started to think like Superman…or like a millionaire.

Here are some of the thoughts you might have during the day:

"The challenges I face day today are easily overcome, after all I am Superman."

"I am indestructible."

"I have incredible strength."

"Nothing can stop me.....NOTHING."

"I have supernatural powers and can overcome anything."

"I can accomplish anything I want when I put my mind to it."

"I can break through any barrier."

"I can and I will do whatever it takes to accomplish my goal."

"I fear nothing."

The trillions of thinking cells in your body and brain listen, and they create exactly what you tell them to create. Their mission is to complete the picture of the you they see and hear when you talk to them. They must obey. It's their job!

Since you are Superman, you cannot fail. Why? Your thinking cells are now sending out the right signal, because you told them to. They are making you stronger, more successful, everyday! You have the ability to fight off all negativity, doubt, fear, and worry—nothing can stop you!

Superman has total confidence. So, your cells of emotion relating to confidence will now create more neuro peptide chemicals to promote feelings of power and confidence that others will feel in your presence.

Superman is fearless. So, your cells of emotion relating to fear will now create more neuro peptide chemicals to create feelings of courage. You are unstoppable!

And here's the key. Others will respond to you in the same way that you are talking to yourself.

If you are confident, others will have confidence in you.

You have thousands of thoughts every day. Make sure your thoughts are leading you in the direction you want to go. Make sure you are telling your cells a success story, and not a 'woe is me' story.

Most have been conditioned to think that creating wealth is difficult, or that it's only for the lucky few. What do you believe? It doesn't cost you any more to think like Superman; and it's much more inspiring!

Mediocrity cannot be an option if you decide to be wealthy and think like Superman.

Your decision, and communication with your cells, creates a mindset; that mindset influences how you show up.

None of that old type of thinking matters anymore…after all, you are Superman and you can accomplish anything.

If you want wealth, you have to stretch yourself. You have to do the things that unsuccessful people are not willing to do. You have to say "yes" to opportunity, then figure out how to get the job done.

Maybe you are uncomfortable selling and asking for money. If that's the case, then learn sales and learn to ask for money every day until you feel comfortable asking for it. You will never have money if you don't learn to ask for it.

I've learned a lot in the past 40+ years as an entrepreneur. I've learned that in order to have more, you have to become more. I've also learned that if you are comfortable, you are not growing. I learned that I couldn't go from a nervous rookie speaker with minimal self-confidence to hosting TV shows and speaking in front of 5,000 people overnight. I simply wasn't ready. I grew into that, one speaking engagement at a time. Every time I finished a speaking engagement, I would ask myself, "How did I do, and how could I do it better?" I still do that today.

And I've learned from the hundreds of thousands of people I've trained, coached, and mentored that none of us can do something we don't believe is possible. It's not going to happen if you're not ready to step out of your comfort zone and stretch yourself.

This has led me to understand the single most important principle of wealth-building, that has meant the difference between poverty and riches for people since humans first traded for pelts.

Are you ready?

Come in just a little closer. Listen up!

Every income level requires a different you! If you think that $10,000 a month is a lot of money, then $100,000 a month will be completely out of reach. If you believe that having $5,000 in the bank would make you rich, then $50,000 won't miraculously appear. You will never earn more money than you believe is "a lot" of money.

What you do as a business is only a small part of becoming rich. In fact, there are thousands, if not tens of thousands, of ways to make money—and lots of it. What I've learned over the years is that, by focusing on who you want to become instead of what you need to do, you're going to multiply your chances of getting rich a hundred-fold.

Ask anyone who's found a way to make a large sum of money legally, and he or she will tell you that it's not hard once you crack the code. And cracking the code starts with you. The "code" to which I refer isn't a secret rite or ancient scroll. It's not even a secret. It's a certain way of thinking and believing in which you've trained your mind to see money-making ideas.

That's where you see a need in the marketplace, and you jump on the idea quickly. It might involve creating a new product; or, it may just be teaching others a special technique you've learned. It may even require raising capital to start a company or to market a product or idea on social media.

Don't hold back. You have to take action to change.

Start right now to imagine yourself as already having wealth. How would your life be? How would your day unfold? Start to own your wealth mindset now! The subconscious mind is unable to differentiate between actual fact and mere visualization. So, by imagining that you already have it, you're encouraging your subconscious mind to seek the ways and means to transform your imaginary feelings into the real thing.

Find yourself some mentors. Nobody has all the answers. Surround yourself with people that will support, inspire, and provide you with answers that keep you moving in the right direction. If you truly want to attain wealth, have a thriving business, or reach the top of your game in any endeavor, having a qualified mentor is essential.

Okay, lets come in for a landing …

It is absolutely essential to have a crystal-clear picture of what you want to accomplish before you begin. If you want to attain wealth, you must learn to operate without fear and with a sharply defined mental image of the outcome you want to attain. This comes from thinking like a wealthy person, (like Superman) making decisions like a wealthy person and being fearless (like Superman) when it comes to stepping out of your comfort zone. Look at the end result as something you're already prepared to do, you just haven't done it yet.

Think about this. Your success is something that you have been preventing; it's not something you have to struggle to make happen. The key is to not let fear, doubt, other people, or mind chatter push your success away. You'll find that the solutions taking you toward your goals will come to you in the most unexpected and sudden ways. You don't need the *perfect* plan first. What you need is a perfectly clear decision about your success, the right mindset, the right mentoring, and the ideal way to get you there will materialize.

The greatest transfer of wealth in the history of the human race is happening right now. Are you positioned to get your share?

Remember, in order to get a different result, you must do something different. In order to do something different you must know something different to do. And in order to know something different, you have to first suspect that your present methods need improving.

THEN, YOU HAVE TO BE WILLING TO DO SOMETHING ABOUT IT.

Eighteen

More Money

"Commitment, that extra resource you draw upon when the going gets tough."
--- Jim Britt

Money is all about freedom. If you want freedom, you'll need plenty of money. So, grow your business, if you have one, as if you're going to sell it for $10 million.

I keep hearing from people about how hard it is to make money. And, yet, I have friends and colleagues that are making money hand over fist, recession or no recession. The money is there to be had no matter what state the economy. There is no less money in the world today than two years ago or two decades ago. People are still spending money—and lots of it.

For you to afford the luxury car you've been lusting after, to spend a full month diving in the Bahamas, or to take the family on some exotic vacation for the entire summer, all you need is a good money-making idea and the willingness to follow some guidance.

NOT making money is hard…wouldn't you agree? If that's the case, then making money must be easy. Here's the really hard part though…*deciding* to make money and sticking to it until it's done; that's the hard part.

You can own a business with dozens of employees, or you can work from home in a network marketing or some other home-based business. It doesn't really matter. If you are in business, the focus should be on making money and avoiding what doesn't make you money.

Ask yourself as you go through the business day, "Is this action making me money, or it is just busyness and tension relieving?" I'm not saying that your whole life should be devoted to making money; it shouldn't at all. But money will give you options as to how you live your life. When you look at your life today, almost every problem you have is brought on from lack of money.

Maybe your passion is to help others. Wouldn't you agree that the more money you earn, the more people you could help? So, if you are marketing a product or service that you feel people need and your passion is to serve others with that product or service, let the amount of money you earn be the gage of how many people you helped.

Do you know what would happen if you just increased your earning by 1% over yesterday? Even if you didn't compound the percentage, in a year you are increasing your earnings by 365%. If you earned $100 today, could you find a way to earn $101 tomorrow? And the more you increase your earnings, the more you'll find ways to use that increase to earn more.

Making more money is all about what you focus on and letting go of what breaks your focus. People fail financially because they have broken their focus. They want to earn more, yet they spend hours a day poking around on social media, hoping some money is going to magically fall into their laps. They fail because they are going off in too many directions. They focus on meaningless stuff, or multiple opportunities at the same time, instead of focusing on a viable opportunity, not listening to every "hot deal" that comes along and sticking with it until it's profitable!

I have a friend. We'll call him Robert. I met Robert around 1990 when he started a business in a direct sales/network marketing company. He went to all the meetings and trainings and had all the knowledge to build the business. He dressed in the finest suits, drove a $50K Mercedes. He had the look of success. With all it appeared he had going for himself he still wasn't earning any money. He was struggling, but he wouldn't give up. I saw him a year later, and he was still struggling.

I ran into him about five years later and asked what he was up to. He said he was still with the same company and earning about $4,000 a month. My thought was that after four years and only earning $4,000 a month, he would never get into the big money that so many others were earning.

Recently, I was on a flight out of LA seated in First-Class. I looked across the aisle and there sat Robert. We were both excited to see one another!

I said, "Man you must be doing okay flying First-Class."

He said, "I always fly first class."

I asked, "What are you up to these days business-wise?" I was shocked when he told me he was still in the same business. Curious, and not wanting to pry into his financial status, I asked, "Well, how is that business going? How big of an organization do you have now?"

Robert responded, "Couple hundred."

I said, "A couple hundred after 30 years?"

He said, "No, a couple hundred thousand in 26 countries."

I was shocked! He went on to tell me that his income was $400,000 monthly, and he had over $36 million in stock he was about to cash in. He also shared with me that he had been using my network marketing training program to grow his business since my program came out over 20 years prior.

Here's the point: find a great opportunity and don't quit just because you don't get rich the first month or year. Getting wealthy takes time. Multiple streams of income are great, but first focus on one until it sustains you financially, then add another. Or, if that one has a lot of potential keep working it.

Bottom line, money is all about freedom. If you want freedom, you'll need plenty of money. So, again, grow your business, if you have one, as if you're going to sell it for $10 million.

Before you do anything, decide right now that you will let go of your old money programming and re-write a new money program that will make you the kind of money that gives you the lifestyle and freedom you want.

To make lots of money you'll need the best possible information on that business regarding how to get started. That can shortcut the time to success. You want to start a business, ask a professional in that business what you need to do to get started and to be successful.

I hear people say all the time, "I don't have a skill set or product to offer." One of my friends presents a 3-day seminar on how to start a business and make money. She charges about $2,000 and guarantees that you will make money with your idea during the class, or she refunds your money. Pretty bold, but 100% of her attendees make money at the class. I attended to see first-hand the results. She had just over 200 people attending and every single person, including me made money during the three-day class. Personally, I walked out with $7000 and won an award for top earner.

My point is, everyone has an idea or a skill that will make them money. Or, for a few hundred dollars, you can join a network marketing company. If you need assistance, I'm happy to recommend a few. Email me at support@jimbritt.com

Hire a mentor, a coach to guide you if needed. Personal development is also important. If you want to develop yourself personally, ask a personal development expert (me), because every life and income level requires a different you. You will need to work harder on yourself than anything else.

In today's marketplace, you'll need mental toughness and a money mindset that helps you overcome obstacles, pushes through self-doubt, and keeps you moving forward. So never stop developing yourself personally. Read uplifting books. Listen to instructional audios. Attend events. You should also have a mentor or coach for ongoing advice, assistance, and encouragement that digs you out of holes and keeps you on course.

You'll need faith too—faith in your decision. Faith that everything is unfolding perfectly.

You'll need to see the truth, the truth behind your actions and results. You'll have to hold yourself accountable for the results you produce, because no one else will. It's easy to have faith that you have a hundred-dollar bill in your hand when you have it in your hand. But you must have faith that your decision to have the money you want will come to you if you let go of your fears, hold true to your decision, take action daily, and hold yourself accountable for your results.

If you want to earn a lot of money you have to have tenacity. You have to stick with it "until." Tenacity is moving forward despite the odds, like my friend Robert. It's moving forward despite what others say. It's moving forward despite what you tell yourself.

Someone asked me a while back, "What do you do when you get down?"

My answer was, "I don't get down. I have been down, and there is nothing down there."

Tenacity is holding true to your commitment until it happens and pulling yourself back up when you get down. If you haven't made a commitment to have the wealth that you say you want, I would encourage you to stop everything right now and not make another move until you are fully committed. I've heard some say, "I am 110% committed." That is a smoke screen, an act, a lie. Why? Because you are either committed, or you are not. No 99% or 110%.

Think about this: what legacy are you leaving by going in your current direction?

Here's a good place to start. First, understand that you no longer want to be just a millionaire.

You want to become a multi-millionaire. While you may think a million dollars will give you financial security, it will not. Given the volatility in economies, governments, and financial markets around the world, it's no longer safe to assume a million dollars will provide you and your family with true security.

In fact, a fidelity investments' study of millionaires in 2017 found that 42 percent of them didn't feel wealthy, and they would need $7.5 million in investable assets to start feeling rich. I'm not talking about a how-to on the accumulation of wealth from a lifetime of saving and pinching pennies. This is about generating multimillion-dollar wealth and enjoying it during the creation process.

To get started, consider these seven secrets of multi-millionaires.

1: Decide to be a multi-millionaire – I've said this may times. If you want a million or more**,** you first have to decide to be a self-made millionaire. I went from nothing, losing everything, my home, both my cars and all my furniture to a millionaire in just one year. The first step is making a decision, setting a target, and taking action.

Think about it. When you make a decision about anything, your view of the world around you changes. Opportunities will show up in your view that you hadn't seen before. Look at it this way. Would you go shop for a new car if you hadn't decided to have one? Would you go on a vacation before you decided to go? No, of course not. Decision always comes first, then the how to.

If you want to be a millionaire, then decide to be one. I mean really decide. I'm talking a firm, unshakable decision, not a hope or a wish. A firm decision that nothing short of a million will do.

I'm not talking about an affirmation, or thinking positive, or hoping the Law of Attraction brings it to you; it won't. What I'm talking about is a decision that doesn't allow for anything less!

No. 2: Get rid of poverty thinking - There's no shortage of money on planet earth, only a shortage of people who think correctly about it and believe they can have it. To become a millionaire from scratch, you must end the poverty thinking right now!

I know because I had to. I was raised in a poor family, by parents who did everything possible to raise four kids and make ends meet. Even though my parents were kind and loving, many of the lessons I learned from my upbringing oftentimes encouraged a sense of scarcity and fear. You've probably heard it, "Eat all your food; there are people starving. Don't waste anything. Money doesn't grow on trees. We can't afford it. There is not enough to go around."

I remember one time, my mother sent me to the corner store to get a box of oatmeal for 23 cents. She handed me a quarter. I asked if I could have 2 cents to buy some candy. (Yes, you could get penny candy when I was a child) I'll never forget when my mother said, "No, you'll need to bring back the change. We will need it for food." We all have programming we need to overcome.

Real wealth and abundance aren't created from this sort of thinking. For many, this type of thinking allows fear to literally run their lives.

Fear of taking a risk.

Fear of the unknown.

Fear of not having enough.

Fear of failure.

Even fear of success.

But fear is a made-up story based on past experience. We then project our made-up story into the future with the anticipation of it happening again…and guess what? It does! Those who engage in this type of thinking usually places the blame on some external factor for their lack of financial success. The positive side of this type of thinking is that you'll always have very little money, so it'll be easy to manage it. ;-)

The good news though, is that you have a choice as to how you think, no matter where you're starting from financially. Begin by looking at the wealth around you. There is no shortage of opportunities to make money, just a shortage of vision. But a person's vision about wealth won't change until they make a decision to become wealthy.

And remember, your attitude about money can be totally different than your current financial reality. In other words, you may not have a lot of money now. That's a reality, not an attitude. The realities may result from certain circumstances. Your attitude about money, on the other hand, reflects how you evaluate what's happening and act upon it. It's not what happens that matters. It's how you perceive it, and what you do about what's happening that's important. Good example. Two partners in business go bankrupt. One jumps out of a ten-story window. The other takes a two-week vacation, regroups, and comes back to launch a new business. Both expressed an attitude. Both had a solution. True story.

Just imagine for a moment that you were a multi-millionaire. How would you act differently? How would you feel? What would your attitude toward money be? Again, most think, "As soon as I make millions, I'll have the attitude of a multi-millionaire." When in fact the opposite is needed—as soon as you start thinking and feeling like a multi-millionaire, only then can you become one.

No. 3: Treat having money like a duty - Self-made multimillionaires are motivated not just by money, but by a need for the marketplace to validate their contributions. For myself, while I have always wanted wealth, I am driven more by my need to contribute consistently to other's lives. Money is a gage of how many I have helped.

Also, multimillionaires don't lower their targets when things get tough. Rather, they raise expectations for themselves because they see the difference they can make with their families, company, community, and charities. They know when they make a contribution to others, the money will follow.

No. 4: Surround yourself with multimillionaires - I have been studying wealthy people since I was 16 years old. I was always intrigued by people that were millionaires or had a lot of money. I always wondered how they did it? In my 20's I started to read their stories and see what they went through, how they made their fortunes. I looked at all of them as my mentors and teachers who inspired me.

I hear all the time that, 'money won't make you happy.' Who says that? I'll tell you who, people without money. Who says, "All rich people are greedy?" I'll tell you who, people who aren't rich. Wealthy people don't think and talk like that. If you want to make a lot of money, you need to know what people are doing, or have done, to create wealth and follow their example.

What do they read?

How do they think?

How do they invest?

What drives them?

Where do they hang out?

How do they stay motivated and excited?

No. 5: Work like a multi-millionaire - Rich people treat time differently. They buy it, while poor people sell it—or even worse, they give it away for pennies or for free. The wealthy know that they can always make more money, but they can't get more time. The wealthy know time is more valuable than money, so they hire people for things they're not good at or that's not a productive use of their time, such as household chores or maintaining the yard.

Look at it this way. You could hire someone to clean your home or mow your grass for $20 an hour. If you decide to do it yourself, just keep in mind that you are working for $20 an hour. But don't kid yourself that those who hit it big financially don't work hard; they do. Financially, successful people are consumed by their hunt for success. They work to the point that they feel they are winning and not just working.

No. 6: Shift your focus from spending to investing -The rich don't spend money; they invest. They spend some of their profits from their investments for luxuries. The poor spend their seed money on a big screen TV and never have money to invest.

The rich know tax laws favor investing over-spending. You personally buy a house and can't write it off except for the interest you pay. The rich incorporate their home and write it off. The rich spend money and pay taxes on what's left, while other people pay taxes and spend what's left, if any. The rich, in contrast, buy an apartment building that produces cash flow, appreciates and offers write-offs year after year.

When you buy cars for comfort and style, that's spending with no write off. The rich, on the other hand, buy cars for their company that are deductible because they are used to produce revenue.

One friend of mine used to refer to spending and investing as "guns" or "butter." When you invest, you load your guns for future profits. When you spend that money on consumer goods its gone, it melts away like butter and never returns. You purchase a TV or other consumer goods, that's butter. You invest in real estate rental properties, that guns. Doesn't mean you don't buy consumer goods, we all do, but most do it with their investment money.

Good philosophy. When you see something you want, ask yourself if you really need it.

If the answer is yes, wait 24 hours before buying it. Your decision may change. You'll be surprised at how many things you thought you needed and then discovered you really didn't. Like going to the supermarket to purchase food when you are hungry. Everything looks good when you are hungry.

No. 7: Create multiple streams of income – The rich never depend on one flow of income but instead create a number of revenue streams. Now, again, you have to be careful with this in the beginning. Don't try to start multiple streams all at one time—that may lead to no streams. Give undivided attention to one, and once that's producing a steady cash flow, start to look at another. Remember, multi-tasking can lead to "multi-getting nothing done." I know people that have been generating a seven-figure income for years before they started investing cash in multifamily real estate or other businesses.

You may also be surprised to learn that wealthy people wish you were wealthy, too. It's a mystery to them why everyone doesn't get rich. They know they aren't anyone special, and that wealth is available to anyone who wants to focus and persist.

Rich people want others to be rich for two reasons:

First, so you can buy their products and services. And second, because they want to hang out with other rich people. So, go ahead and get rich; it's okay to be rich. Whether you're an entrepreneur running a startup, running a department in a large company, or you simply want to live a better lifestyle, more money must become your mantra.

Money is one of those taboo topics in society that most don't like to talk about. On the other hand, we will admire athletes and celebrities and envy them for the money they earn and look up to those who have more. I read that Jerry Seinfeld, in the early 2000's, earned 279 million in one year, and since then, has been earning about 86 million a year. And he's selling comedy! Funny uh? Who would have thought you could earn that much money just joking around.

The poor people criticize him for making so much money. They criticize because they are not willing to go through what I'm sure he went through to get rich. I actually always loved Seinfeld.

Think about it…the idea of wanting "more money" is a bad thing only with those who don't have enough of it. When you want to expand your business and some unplanned emergency comes along, or you need more money to donate to your favorite cause, politically correct sayings about money will not help you; only more money will help you.

Big question…does money buy happiness? The fact is that wealthier people are happier than poor people. Wealthier countries are happier than poor countries. I personally don't think that money will make you happy, but it seems as people earn more, they become happier. The relationship between income and happiness is extremely strong. Maybe a better word for it would be pleasure vs happiness. Money lets you enjoy more of the pleasures life has to offer. A new BMW won't make you happy, but it is more of a pleasure to drive than a Ford Focus. It won't make you happy, but it will allow you to get to your problems in style and comfort.

Now I'm not saying to spend all your waking hours going after more money. What sense does that make? Then you wouldn't have any time left to enjoy your life's pleasures. All I'm saying is, embrace the idea that having more is a good thing, not a bad thing. So, start today to set your mind on having all you need to live the life you want.

On the other hand, there is no point in having money just for the sake of having money.

Money for money's sake never works. But money used to start a business is good. Money donated to a cause is good. Money to have fun with is good. Money to relieve stress and worry is good. Whether it be for a boat or traveling the world, for a new car or fine food and wine, it's all good. It's all well spent and is certainly better than money left sitting in a bank for the sake of having more. There is nothing wrong with ambition, or with attaining wealth, provided that wealth is used for something good that enhances your life and the lives of those around you.

Here are some reasons why more money should be a must for you, your family, and your business:

1. The alternative sucks! The opposite of more money is not having enough money, or worse, being broke. I have first-hand experience with both. Not having money sucks. When you lack money, you're unable to grow a business or do the things you want to do while you are here on the planet. Operating without enough money is like driving a car with the emergency brake engaged. You need more money to release that brake!

2. Earning money is a whole lot easier than being broke. When you are broke, you spend all your time and energy trying to figure out how to survive. The end result is you survive. But what if you spend the same amount of time and energy actually focused on earning more instead of just enough for survival?

Think about it. You get what you focus on 100% of the time. Survival = survival. I think you'll agree that earning money is a whole lot easier than being broke. Being broke is hard. It'll drain your time, energy, creativity, happiness, and keep you from enjoying some of the pleasures in life. Having money lets you live life on your own terms.

3. You'll out-live your money. The old saying, "life is short" may apply to some things, but when it comes to money, life is too long for most. People today are more likely to out-live their money. Retirement is the single biggest money concern today. Nobody wants to be a drain on anyone else. As life expectancies extend, your financial requirements must also extend; so don't wait.

4. Inflation is a thief. The cost of food, gas, education, insurance, housing, and running a business are increasing daily. Inflation is an invisible thief. It's called the "hidden tax" because you don't see it in the money you earn, but you do see it in the money you spend. Earning more money is the only way to combat inflation.

5. Prove the naysayers wrong. One of the driving forces in my life has been proving the naysayers wrong. Yes, I admit, it's a bit immature, but there is nothing better than a sense of accomplishment in the face of those that counted you out. As my life-long friend and business partner, Jim Rohn, used to say, "The best revenge is massive success."

6. There is no shortage of money. Machines make money, and there is no shortage of how much those machines can make. To think that you can't get your share is ridiculous when you consider that there is about $50 trillion dollars in global circulation. There is a greater shortage of people going for more money than there is a shortage of money. Sounds like a simplification, but my entire financial world changed when I realized there was no shortage except for the money shortage in my mind.

7. Someone else will get it. Somebody is going to end up with your money if you don't make a claim to it. Most importantly, why should it not be you? People complain about not having enough money, but most people are not staking a claim to what's theirs. Money circulates from person to person, and it wants to be active! It wants YOU to have it!

8. Money is freedom! You and I don't go to work to make money. We go to work each day with the purpose of creating freedom for our family and ourselves. Yet 90% of the population doesn't have the money to enjoy much level of freedom. Most wealthy people enjoy the freedom money provides them. Financial freedom provides you with the ability to try new things, make new investments, and have more choices about how to live your life.

9. You deserve more money. When I understood that I deserved money as much as anyone else—and that more money did not turn me into some evil, greedy person—I started earning more money. So, start right now, today, and commit to getting rid of all limiting beliefs and ideas that may be blocking you from having the money you deserve. "More money" should be your mantra, and there's nothing wrong with that if it's for the right reason—which is enjoying more freedom.

Your comfort zone is the enemy of wealth and freedom. Think of all you want in life that you can't have right now because of lack of money. Then decide to go out and get the money to have it.

UNLIMIT YOURSELF! GO AHEAD, STEP UP, STEP OUT, AND TAKE CENTER STAGE.

Nineteen

The Millionaire Maker's Attitude

"Our real problems in life arise not from what happens to us, but rather from our worries and demands of what we think should be happening to us."

--- Jim Britt

So, what exactly is attitude?

Your attitude takes in, digest, uses, or rejects what is valuable and what is not, based on how you see yourself.

Your attitude is like a command post.

I'll try or I won't try.

I'll learn or I won't learn.

I'll make the call, or I'll put it off.

I'll take advantage of an opportunity, or I'll let it pass me by.

Your attitude influences your behavior and the behavior of those around you. In other words, like a mindset, attitude determines how you show up to the world and how the world shows up to support you.

Attitude is defined as, 'A mental position or feeling with regard to something else.'

Maintaining the right attitude will be one of the most essential parts of self-management and wealth building. Attitude is not something that you just turn on when you face a prospect, then turn off when you leave them. Your attitude is a reflection of who you are and what you honor in your life. Your attitude is a mindset.

What happens, happens to everyone. The very same circumstances can happen to two different people and yet one comes out on top while the other gets caught up in their circumstances. Both express their attitude.

Attitude is the starting point for everything good or not so good. Your attitude is the mechanism that turns on or shuts off the flow of ideas that can bring forth your success. With the right attitude you'll become a powerful beacon, a human magnet for attracting pleasant experiences and creating the things you want in life.

Your attitude toward your clients or prospects will determine their attitude toward you and your products or services. Your attitude toward life will determine how life treats you. Your attitude toward your business will determine how the business provides for you financially.

So, it's vitally important to develop a resourceful, aspiring attitude.

Aspire to do well in business.

Aspire to give good service.

Aspire to follow-up and assist your customers.

Aspire to help others become successful.

Aspire to have people like you and want to be a member of your team.

Aspire to be non-judgmental toward yourself and others.

Aspire to communicate well and have people listen to you.

Aspire to listen to others with sincere interest.

Aspire to present yourself well.

Aspire to become a great leader.

Aspire to become a leader of leaders.

Aspire to have an inspiring attitude!

Aspire to have people feeling better after having contact with you.

There is a huge difference however, between expecting these things and aspiring to have them happen. Expectation will almost always end in disappointment. When you expect something to happen in a certain way, at a certain time and it doesn't, you are always disappointed.

Aspiring to do something leaves you room to be flexible. If you aspire to reach the stars and only hit the moon, it's still okay. You are not disappointed because you did your best. You can aspire to do your best and allow others to be their best in your presence. On the other hand, when you expect to be <u>THE</u> best, you compete with everyone in your presence.

I've found that more times than not we always get exactly what we truly aspire to have in our lives. The reason is that aspiration begins with what you honor in your life. What you honor is like a value you aspire to live by. Some may not have the same values as you. And if you expect them to have your values you will be disappointed every time.

The results of your attitude will always show up in the bottom line. It will show up in the success of your business. It will show up in your bank account. It will show up in your overall happiness. The result of your attitude will show up in every area of your life.

Here are a few simple points that will help in maintaining the right attitude.

Continue to refine and develop your **compelling why**. Why do you want what you want? You want to earn a lot of money…why?

Continue to refine the reasons you are seeking wealth, or whatever you seek. This should be a constant refining process of holding true to the real essence of why you do what you do. Then, develop and implement a clear-cut strategy plan that will lead you toward achieving your compelling why.

Next is to develop a **strong conviction** about the value of what you have to offer. Your conviction will always come across in your presentation, in your attitude. If you are not sold on the value of what you offer, how could we ever expect someone else to be sold?

Remember your first love affair and how you felt? Fall in love with your business the same way. Treat your business like a love affair.

Fall in love with the financial potential of your business.

Fall in love with your team spirit.

Fall in love with the value of your products or services.

Fall in love with the challenge of being your best.

Fall in love with being a good leader.

Fall in love with being a leader of leaders.

Fall in love with working on yourself and your personal growth.

Fall in love with the opportunity to make a difference in someone else's life.

Next have a **do it now** attitude. Develop a sense of urgency, not a sense of panic. You simply know exactly what you want to accomplish, and you get the job done without hesitation. Look for reasons to do it now instead of putting it off until later.

Next, **create a plan** for your own development. Your income will not far exceed your personal growth. A person will always create exactly what they believe they are worth. Therefore, working on your own development and sense of self-worth will always pay great dividends. You earn what you believe you are worth. Read constructive books, listen to audios, attend live training events. Remember, change and growth happen one idea at a time.

Next, **become a risk taker.** Many look for the risk in the opportunity and by doing so they may miss the opportunity altogether. Instead, develop the attitude of looking for the opportunity in the risk. Talking to strangers is risky. They might say no! Instead, look for the opportunity in the risk. Look for all the reasons they might say yes and focus your efforts on those things.

Next, **be innovative.** Always keep an open mind to new ideas and possibilities. What if you try something new and it doesn't work? What have you gained? You've gained experience, right? On the other hand, what if you don't try something new and it would have worked? What have you gained? Nothing! Be open to trying new things, new methods, until you discover what works best for you. Remember that your attitude is contagious both to yourself and to others!

When it comes to earning money, I find that there are basically six different types of attitudes that will determine the level of success you achieve.

The poverty attitude. This is what's known as the lower income attitude. This type can't fully commit to a given opportunity for any period of time because fear literally runs their lives. They jump from opportunity to opportunity, sometimes even working three or four at the same time. They are hoping that one of them will make enough money to pay their bills each month, and that's about all they can ever expect.

The person with this attitude seems to always place the blame on someone or something else for their lack of success. "I don't get enough support. The products are too expensive. I live in a small town. Nobody I know has money." All low income excuses. This attitude encourages a state of dependence. The good part is that they have little or no money, so they really don't have to worry about managing it.

The paycheck-to-paycheck attitude. This one is a step up from the poverty attitude. This type of person is always looking for job security and will take very few risks. This attitude restricts personal initiative. This type of person may even become bitter toward someone who is doing well or who breaks out of this attitude. They let fear run their lives—fear of stepping out of their comfort zone, fear of doing anything that might jeopardize their paycheck.

The middle income attitude. It is the existence of this one that has allowed free enterprise to thrive with a maximum amount of growth and freedom. This is usually a healthy attitude; they accept reality as it is. They usually experience some degree of growth throughout their life. The only problem with this type is that their attitude toward money does not always prepare them to take the risks necessary to move to new levels financially. Those with this attitude usually end up spending their money for some kind of get-rich-quick scheme that rarely makes any money. They also have the capacity to open up whole new exciting opportunities for financial growth. They are also open to coaching.

The game player attitude. This is the middle-income attitude that, through coaching, can be raised to a higher level. This person takes someone else's game and plays it to the maximum. Instead of earning $100,000 a year, he or she may be earning $200,000 to 300,000 a year. Over time, they also can develop the skills to earn even higher incomes. They usually take risks, but usually with some degree of caution and only within their area of expertise.

The game maker attitude. This type can create their own game or play someone else's for a piece of the action. These people usually create a lot of wealth for themselves and others. They see themselves as a partner with everyone on their team. They are as much concerned about the success of each team member as they are their own success. They will spend a lot of time and energy accomplishing their objectives. The person with this attitude has a lot of self-confidence and usually makes a lot of money.

The millionaire-maker's attitude. This is the one we all want to concentrate on and develop. We all have the ability to do so no matter where we are starting from financially or what experience we have in business. This attitude actually frees you from money and allows you to experience life from a whole new perspective. This attitude puts money in its place and lets you concentrate your efforts on your business, helping others around you achieve success and live life to the fullest. The pleasures and freedom this attitude brings forth is unlimited. The important thing to know is that it is not limited to those who already have money, a vehicle, or the skill of making money. Anyone can develop this attitude no matter what their circumstances or financial condition.

How do you develop this attitude? You begin by looking at the wealth around you. What would you think of someone who had millions and complained of being broke? You'd probably have very little sympathy for them, wouldn't you? Yet many people act this way because they don't see the wealth around them. Money is everywhere. Opportunities to make money are everywhere! All you have to do is develop the attitude necessary to recognize and go after these opportunities. The very first step is to use your imagination. Take all those old thoughts, feelings, and beliefs you have developed about money over the years, and if you are not satisfied with them, toss them out! Let them go! You no longer need them! Stop focusing on them!

It's also important to remember that your attitude toward money can be totally different from the reality of how things actually are in your life. You may not have money now, but that is a reality not an attitude. The realities in your life are a result of your past actions, and at this point, it just is what it is. You can't change what happened. You can't change your current circumstances. Your attitude, on the other hand, reflects ways in which you evaluate what is happening and how to change it. As I said before, it's not what happens to you that matters. It's what you do about what happens that counts. That's an attitude. To develop the millionaire makers attitude, you need to begin to see yourself as already having millions. Imagine for a moment that you had all the money you ever wanted.

Most seem to get stuck in the attitude that, "As soon as I make some money, I'll start living the life I want." By doing so, you deny yourself the opportunities and pleasures that are right in front of you. We just can't see them because of our tunnel vision, spending all our time focused on the problem.

The point I'm trying to make is for you to begin to think and act as if you already have money. Act as if money is no longer a problem in your life. Act as if you have the power and freedom that comes with having money. If you made a million dollars in your business, how would you come across? Would you be different? If so, then start acting that way and see what it will do for your effectiveness. If you seem desperate, your prospects will smell it and feed your desperation with a "no."

There is a very unusual thing that happens. People often value what they don't have more than what they do have. A person without money would value him/herself more if he or she had money. Every time you envy someone else, or become depressed because you don't have certain things while others do, you actually move your center of power away from your strength. This attitude will result in becoming weak and having a feeling of insecurity. Before you can ever have millions, your attitude will have to be one of valuing where you are right now, while moving toward where you want to be.

The number one secret to developing a millionaire's attitude is to value yourself. Place no one else above you. What I mean is, stand face to face on an equal level with anyone, no matter what their level of wealth and success. You value and enjoy your own life because you are putting forth your best. When you value yourself, your true value will show through to others and people will want to support you. With this attitude, when you come in contact with another, you will carry a presence that will be powerful and effective. By having this attitude, you can eliminate your struggles right now! In your mind, you can reach whatever wealth figure makes you feel secure. You can begin to feel content and secure with whatever money you have, and then start to act like you already have what you want. The quality of your life should not ever depend on how much money you have. Good health, relationships, family, and pleasure all operate outside the world of money. You become a millionaire by learning to seek out and enjoy the things you want in life. However, you can move this attitude into a state of being a millionaire. Don't forget. It is the personal development, the person you become <u>mentally and emotionally,</u> that brings peace of mind and wealth into your life. One of the most important things you can do for your business is to work harder on yourself than you do on anything else.

Self-management starts with learning from experience, both yours and others. If you host a business meeting, you will get results and you will learn from your experience. If you observe someone else hosting a business meeting, you will learn from observing them. If you talk to people, some will respond favorably, and some will not. You will learn from both. If you share your products or services, some will become customers, some will not. Learn from both and you can gain clarity about what to do and what not to do to acquire new customers in the future. If you follow-up, you'll get results. The more you observe the actions that produced results, the better the results you will attain in the future. If you give full support to your team members, they will duplicate the process and your business will grow. If you work on yourself, your value as an individual will grow, and you will become an example for others to follow. Activity always produces results! However, the quality of your activity, and the result that follow, will be determined by your attitude. Self-management simply means being a monitor of your own actions and constantly asking yourself:

HOW DID I DO IT, AND HOW COULD I HAVE DONE IT BETTER?

Twenty

Control Your Focus

"The degree of clarity, focus, and commitment toward a desired outcome will determine the speed and the degree of accuracy of the results produced."

--- Jim Britt

People become immobilized when they have broken their focus. Everyone has a focus, but the real question is, what are you focused on? Either you control your focus or your broken focus controls you. If you turn on the TV or radio, all you hear is a lot of media nonsense; they are ultimately all about controlling your focus. Every day there's a different drama about something that people forget in 3 days anyway (most of the time). Yes, there's some real negative stuff out there like terrorism, economy, politics, and more. But if you focus on those things, you become part of the problem instead of finding a solution to living the life you want. If you can do something to help a situation, do it. But if there is nothing you can do, but vote or write your congressperson, do it. That's why this message is more important than ever. Because again, either you control your focus or the world will snatch it right away from you.

We're living in a world where there is no such thing as 'job security' anymore. There's just not.

We're living in a society that, unless you take ownership of your focus, your skills, and your attitude, you're in deep trouble…really deep trouble.

Everyone is after your focus. Can you feel it? Start to observe day-to-day and you'll see what I mean. See how many times during the day someone tries to control what you focus on. You'll be shocked when you really become aware of it. The other day, I was watching the Today Show while working out. In one hour, I counted 11 commercials on prescription drugs. They advertise to get you to call your doctor and request one of their prescriptions. UNBELIEVABLE! Especially given the fact that most of these drugs kill more people than auto accidents and wars combined. I'm not saying that prescription drugs are all bad. For some, it may save their life, but at least educate yourself because the side effects could kill you! Will you submit to ridiculous input like this that steals your focus and takes you away from what you want and really need? Or will you rise up and take control?

Listen, I know procrastination may be kicking your butt right now. It kicks everyone's now and then. And yes, you're probably having a problem with inconsistency also. I might even add in a bit of perfectionism as well. "Everything has to be just right, then I'll get going." Been there, done that. Now is your time to take the next step forward. Doesn't have to be a big step, just a small one. Just start with one small step toward financial freedom. That's all you need right now to make progress. It's time to take ownership of your focus and take action on your wealth plan. Because what you choose to focus on with all your passion and persistence will, in fact, be created. You can watch it happen. The universe is a mirror that reflects back exactly what you are putting out. Anything you want is all yours if you choose to control your focus. That's just the reality. The bullet train of time and wealth is leaving the station and you have a ticket. Will you focus and take the ride of your life or watch it leave the station?

You are important.

You are special and unique.

You are fearless.

You are more powerful than you know. Much more.

You were born to be great. Much greater than you think.

You were born to build a masterpiece called your life.

We've all had challenges.

We've all made mistakes.

We've all procrastinated too much.

We've all had a bad year.

We've all been way too scattered at times.

Big deal. That was then, this is now!

Your future is as bright, lively, and fun as you make it, so embrace it. Go ahead. Life doesn't happen to you. It happens for you! So why not make every day your best ever! Every day is your chance to move forward into an abundant lifestyle—if you decide what you want and control your focus. You were born with a gift, wrapped and all. A unique gift. Now it's your job to find it and share it with the world. That decision is yours, not mine.

Don't get in the box

So, you say you don't have a product or service to sell. Or you don't have a business. Or you have a business and want to add a second stream of income. Think outside the box! Better yet, don't get in the box. You've no doubt heard of 6 Degrees of Separation. The 6 Degrees of Separation state that the levels where everyone is connected are no more than 6. All niche markets, to some degree, are related as well. Not from context to products, but of people in context to themselves. In other words, if someone is interested in hiking shoes, they might also be interested in camping equipment, skiing equipment, or fishing gear. And it doesn't necessarily have to be about a product you are selling. They can be about related interests as well. Someone interested in boating may also be interested in diving. Someone interested in bicycling may be interested in fitness, exercise equipment, or nutritional supplements. So, do you see my point. Just about any activity, hobby, profession, product, or interest could be only a few levels away from many others. That's why affiliate, social media, and internet marketing can be so powerful. Affiliate marketing is where you contract with someone to sell their products and you earn a percentage. Or, it could be the other way around. Maybe someone else would be interested in selling your product for a percentage.

Even if you are not coming at it from the angle of selling additional products, knowing related interests can give you some common language that you can use to build the relationship, like you would do in maybe a network marketing business model. Take the time to figure out what these relationships are from a product aspect, as well as an interest aspect. By doing so, you might add many other products or services to your campaign.

Here are a few focus tips.

1. Focus on the current economic times and use it to your advantage. Money is still out there, and people are spending it too. Maybe not the unemployed, but for sure those who are employed. These people still need your products or services.

Even the unemployed and under employed need certain products or services. That, in part, is the reason I created Cracking the Rich Code www.CrackingTheRichCode.com and The Rich Code Club, www.TheRichCodeClub.com. Those needing to find a better way have the opportunity to learn how to take control of their own financial future instead of leaving it to someone else or to chance.

Here's a great example: I recently met a young man that was earning over a million dollars a year marketing on the internet and social media. I asked him what his product was, and he said, "I sell classic Mustang parts." Curious, I asked if he had a warehouse somewhere where he stored and shipped the parts from. He said, "Oh, no, I have never seen a Mustang part. I sell other people's Mustang parts." He had also added other products that those in the market for these parts might buy, like car wax, custom wheels, floor mats, and radar detectors.

Another friend who speaks Spanish started marketing motivational audio programs to the Spanish market through Click Bank. He was the #1 marketer on click bank for two years in a row.

If you are looking to become an affiliate marketer, Click Bank has hundreds, if not thousands, of affiliate products to choose from. They will even provide the marketing copy to use to sell it.

2. Focus on today. The past is the past, and you can't change that. Learn from it, yes, but don't focus on it. Enough said.

3. Focus on opportunities, trends, timely products that could be marketed on the internet and social media. The greatest transfer of wealth is happening right now, and you can have your share.

4. Focus on streamlining your business by outsourcing tasks like fulfillment, accounting, web design, etc. Outsource tasks that can be done by others costs you less than your time is worth. If you are just starting out, don't worry too much about accounting. When you have something to account, then hire an accountant, or use quick books, or both.

5. Focus on being bold. Step out of your comfort zone and try something different. If you are afraid to market on the internet, find a product, become an affiliate, or join a network marketing company, and give it a go. You might be pleasantly surprised by the results you produce. I have been getting residual checks from 2 network marketing companies for years, and I haven't worked for them for years.

6. Focus on daily, even hourly results. Ask yourself at the end of every day, or hour, "Did my last day (or hour) move me in the direction of my objective?" Best success habit I know.

7. Focus on a strategy plan for the day. Know what you are going to do and when, then do it. Don't get sidetracked by tension relieving tasks like scrolling on social media. Focus only on goal achieving tasks.

8. Focus on making money. Being in business is about making money, so focus on revenue producing activities. For most of us, that is going to be marketing and sales. Finding a way to get in front of new prospects should be 80% of your efforts.

9. Focus on thinking big! Operate at your highest level of productivity possible each day. Know what you are going to do and don't be timid. Act and feel as if you already have made your fortune!

10. Focus on finding the parade that's trending and put yourself in front of it.

Stay ahead of the curve with new information, trends, education, and opportunities, especially on the internet. The great thing about the internet and affiliate marketing is that you can do it from anywhere. Internet marketing gives you an opportunity to profit from industries you may never have had access to before. Think outside the box. You can take your message to your exact target customers through social media like Facebook, Twitter, Instagram, LinkedIn and others. Watch for what's hot, a growing trend or a new industry, or maybe a shift in technology. Then, be quick to look into it and adapt.

Financial success is about making progress, the smartest way you can, so you get maximum rewards for the time and talent you invest. The increased money is just an added bonus.

Just for fun, go onto the internet and find out what's trending. Go to twitter.com and read the scroll line that moves across the screen that says "trending." Or go to yahoo.com and read the top ten list of what's trending. Look for what's online and what's trending in technology, sales, clothing, you name it. Then, think outside the box and brainstorm how you can take advantage of new trends, technology and info online, and use new online marketing techniques to help you achieve success.

Earning more money is always trending. People are looking for ways to earn more. If you like what you gain in this book, or one of my programs at www.jimbritt.com, we have an affiliate program as well. You can become a Cracking the Rich Code affiliate.

Will you sit on the bench or step up to the plate and hit one out of the park?

BATTER UP! NOW SWING!

Twenty-one

Letting Go of the Need to Control

"Create your vision and play with whoever shows up to play."

--- Jim Britt

Imagine for a moment how much time is required to travel 250,000 light years—that's traveling at the speed of light, 186,000 miles per second, for 250,000 years. That's hard to imagine, isn't it? A single galaxy is estimated to be that far across. Now imagine a galaxy that is four galaxies away from Earth. That's 1,000,000 light years away. There are billions of galaxies within the universe. It's hard to imagine, isn't it?

Now imagine in the center of our galaxy is planet Earth, where we live. Compared to the universe, or even our galaxy, Earth is pretty small stuff, right? Now imagine yourself on Earth. Even smaller stuff, aren't you? Now imagine your problems that you try so hard to control. Pretty small stuff, isn't it?

I have a theory. When we arrive here on Earth, we are given an allotment of "cosmic energy" to burn up, and when it's gone, our trip gets canceled. We can decide how to burn up our energy.

For example, let's say you are traveling down the highway at seventy mph. You're going to an appointment five miles away, and if you continue at the same speed, you'll arrive on time with a couple minutes to spare. All of a sudden, you get cut off by someone who decides to travel at only sixty mph. You begin to get uptight. "How could this idiot be in front of me? Doesn't he have a brain or what?" If you continue at the same speed for the remainder of your five miles, that idiot will have cost you about thirty seconds. Thirty seconds is not the issue. The real issue is how much of your "cosmic energy" allotment you have used. To what degree did your "need to control" something that is not within your control shorten your time on Earth? Maybe a minute, and hour, or maybe you are so uptight it's your last minute?

Or, imagine this—you go into the bathroom, and at that critical moment, you realize that there's no toilet tissue. You have a choice to make. Do you yell and scream at the kids for not refilling? Do you want to burn up some of your "cosmic energy" allotment for this? It's alright if you do, but it's really good to know who's making the decisions.

You are having an argument with your spouse, and you're getting pretty angry. There are two things you might want to consider. First, you might want to ask yourself, "Who really wins in an argument?" The second thing is, "Do I want to burn a portion of my energy allotment for this, or is there a more sane, stress-free solution?"

Our emotional stress doesn't come from the situation. It comes from our trying to control and manipulate the situation into something it's not. We suffer physically when something is not working properly in our bodies. We suffer emotionally when something is not working in concert with the way we believe it should. We suffer mentally when we don't get what we want, or when we feel forced to live with something we don't want. Mental and emotional suffering has been shown to cause physical suffering. In fact, it is believed to be the root cause of most illness, so why engage?

Whatever you feel, think, speak, or observe is always in a constant state of change. By remaining in a non-observant state of mind, not being "mind-full," this change will register as dissatisfaction in your life. We then increase the problem by trying to stop the change from happening. We want to fix things. We try to control and manipulate something that can't be controlled. We even attempt to control it internally, by conceptualizing how we wish the situation to be. We want everything to be concrete in our minds so that we can have a sense of direction, meaning, and control.

Even if you attempt to make your situation a little more bearable by manipulating it, before long, it will be back in a state of flux once again, causing you more suffering. Why? Because trying to control something that is beyond your control leaves you out of control! It becomes painful because it's your attempt to change reality.

As an example, let's say you are thirty days behind on a project you need to complete. No matter how hard you try, or how much you wish your circumstances were different, it's not going to change the reality of your situation, that you are thirty days behind.

By becoming a "mind-full" observer, you can see the situation clearly. You can now choose not to try to control something that can't be controlled. You can choose not to burn up your energy. Most importantly, you can now take action to change your situation from a place of resourcefulness, versus a place of anxiety, which will get you nowhere.

Attempting to manipulate the world, our business affairs, relationships, other people, and situations is the number one source of suffering and non-productivity. Until we see this, and experience it to be true, our number one priority will always be to control uncontrollable situations. What we don't realize is that in our attempt to be in control, all we are doing is creating more suffering and lack of control. Whatever we attempt to control, controls us.

You may be broken. That's a reality you can't change. However, you can control how you respond to the situation and what you can do in the next moment to change your situation. So many people focus on the, "I am broken" trying to control how they feel and how they got there, that they miss all the opportunities coming their way to change their situation. There is only one way out of the "maze," and it's not through control. It's by seeing our situation for what it is, instead of what we wish it would be.

Try this exercise: picture a triangular circle. Got it? Of course not, it's impossible, isn't it? Very often we spend our allotment of energy trying to do similar things. We focus our efforts on things that are next to impossible to control.

We often think that if we just put forth a lot of effort, we will accomplish more and change our circumstances, when exactly the opposite is true. Correct effort is the key. This sort of action involves no struggle, no pushing, no forcing, because correct effort means being in direct alignment, with a clear view of our objective and a clear view of reality. Only then do you have a clear view of what to do next.

Suppose you place your thumb on top of a nail, then hit it with a hammer. You wouldn't need to force yourself to keep from doing it again, would you? The reality is, it hurts! Correct view lets you know how to avoid the pain of doing it the incorrect way again. Correct view and correct effort mean simply being present in whatever you are doing right here, right now. It's not about trying to control by making a situation into something it's not. All that does is create more stress and use up more energy. Stress burns energy. There is no stress in the moment… unless, of course, you bring it into the moment.

We've all been taught that effort requires control. Human history is filled with this sort of approach. Take a look around at the world we've spent a great deal of our effort and energy trying to control. We've controlled our land, environment, waterways, and even society to the point that we are now wondering whether the human race will even survive! Does that give you any indication that being controlling doesn't work? If you want to bring about change in the world, in your life, you must focus your efforts on two things. The first is vision. How would you like your world to be? Second, is reality. What are you trying to control that can't be controlled, that's burning up your creative energy?

By becoming self-observant, you will discover that your mental and emotional state is fragmented with thoughts and feelings such as, "Am I going to get what I want? I don't like the way I feel. Why is this person out to get me? Why is life so difficult?" Your real efforts should be turned toward letting go of such thoughts and feelings. Attempting to drive them away by controlling them, only strengthens their position and staying power. If you simply back off and observe your fragmented state, and see it for what it is, rather than feeding it by pushing it away, or wanting reality to be something different, then you once again return to a resourceful state where correct action can be taken.

Your clear vision cannot be manifested without taking correct action. As an example, if you go to your vehicle, open the door, get in, sit down, and think about starting your car, nothing happens. The correct action that creates the desired outcome is pushing the starter button and actively driving the car. Clear vision creates an energy of "aliveness," and lack of action toward that vision creates stress. The correct use of energy constitutes action. The misuse of energy creates stress.

We all need our peaceful thoughts and times of non-action, but they are much less valuable than ideas backed up by correct action. Think success, of course. This is always the first step in achieving success. The next step, however, is to go beyond thinking to implementation. By combining vision with correct action, we can take success or anything else, to a whole new level. Attempting to control that which is out of our control creates anxiety, and anxiety is a short circuit in the manifestation process, because there is no stable thought or action to rely upon.

If you look back over your life, you could probably come up with a long list of failures you've had or of people who have hurt you in some way. We all have our list. The parent, the schoolteacher, the husband, the wife, the child, the best friend, the business partner, the list is endless. Because of this list of failures and pains, we then develop patterns of avoidance, which cause us to develop a conditioned way of thinking and perceiving life. We develop behavior patterns of avoidance, trying desperately to avoid our own self-created pain!

We begin to judge and fear others. We judge ourselves. We form opinions about anyone or anything we fear that might cause us any sort of pain. Most of us spend our whole lives attempting to move in a direction that avoids discomfort. We believe that we are the victims, so we attempt to arrange our entire lives so that we are in control; but without even realizing it, what we are really doing is setting up a life that is out of control. We have become so obsessed with not being hurt and remaining in control, that our real lives are just passing us by without notice. We spend 90% of our time defending our needs.

Our methods for avoiding pain have become almost endless. When we are threatened in any way, we instantly react by putting up a barrier of some sort that we hope will keep us in control. But in reality, what is really happening is that we are clouding our vision with our need to control something beyond our control. Because most of us are in a reactive state every few minutes, or even seconds, our vision of how we want our lives to be, or how life really is, is completely out of focus.

If you want to create wealth and avoid stress and inner conflict, the key is to learn to distinguish between things we can control and those we cannot. In other words, learn to identify the difference between controllable and uncontrollable circumstances.

Any circumstance that is beyond your control is not your responsibility. If, however, there is an action that should or could be taken, you should first let go of your need to control the outcome, then take action. By doing so you truly remain in control of your thoughts, feelings, emotions and behaviors. All of these things can burn up your allotment of energy, which is the only thing you really have control of in the first place. If there is no action to take, you should simply let go of your need to control and have the courage to leave it at that.

Concerning yourself with what others think, or how something should turn out, is a non-resourceful leak of your resourceful energy. Whatever happens that is beyond your control, should simply be accepted as a necessary part of the overall process. A seemingly non-resourceful event may just be taking place for the purpose of keeping you in a certain place long enough for the real event to happen, or to give you the opportunity to let go of your need for control—or both.

When you let go of the need to control outcomes, you don't actually give up control at all, or give up using any of your skills. What you really give up is using your skills to manipulate your world and the people in your life by trying to make them the way you would like them to be. You then create a sense of peace, joy, and flow in your life.

DON'T SWEAT THE SMALL STUFF. WHEN YOU WERE BORN WAS BIG STUFF! WHEN YOU DIE WILL BE BIG STUFF. EVERYTHING IN BETWEEN IS SMALL STUFF.

Twenty-two

Breaking Habits That No Longer Serve You

"Perhaps if we stopped hanging onto outdated beliefs and beating ourselves up for it, there would be no reason to continue the behavior that leads to the beating."

--- Jim Britt

A habit is any action that you have performed so often it becomes almost an involuntary response, or second nature. As I mentioned in a previous chapter, we have positive habits that become second nature, like walking or driving an automobile. We also have negative habits that become second nature, like the man that couldn't pay his bills on time for twenty-five years. In most cases we don't even know we are engaging in them. That's what we are all trying so hard to break free from. If you consider a habit to be undesirable, like smoking or overeating or being stuck in a rut financially, then you may label it a bad habit.

People spend countless hours and dollars each year attempting to break these bad habits and often without much success. Why? Because there is no magic bullet. Change is hard work and there is no short cut except to do it. The steps a person needs to take, however, can be very simply outlined.

To effect a change in habits, you first need to bring action back into the realm of consciousness and regain the ability to make choices. In other words, you have to become aware that you are engaging in the habit and make a conscious choice not to engage.

Payoff or Tradeoff

The first step in breaking a bad habit is to look at why you find this action so compelling. In other words, what's the payoff for doing this seemingly negative thing? Since you've already classified this as a "bad" habit, you may be tempted to say there isn't a payoff. But, if you look closer, you'll find the payoff. There is always a payoff.

Let's say you are in sales and your bad habit is not following up. What's your payoff? You get to avoid the possible rejection of a "No." The payoff could be that you get to spend more time on the Internet doing things that make it seem like you are busy or simply that you get to avoid the pain of possible rejection!

On the other hand, now, take a look at the tradeoff. What is it that you are losing by exercising your habit? This step should be easier. Just think about why you consider it a bad habit in the first place. For example, not following up is a bad habit, because if you continue, you'll end up with no results. You are trading the temporary release of staying busy for something that produces nothing. Now that you've weighed both sides of the issue—your payoff and your tradeoff—it's time to make a choice. Once you are aware that you have this bad habit, it's no longer an involuntary act; you know you are making a conscious choice every time you perform this action. You are choosing what you value more…the *payoff* or the *tradeoff!*

It's Either Black or White

You see, we live in a black and white world, not a gray world. You may say, "Well, I don't always follow up, but most of the time I do. Besides, a little of not following isn't that bad." That's the gray answer most use to justify why they keep engaging in the bad habit. The reality is, it is a black and white choice to engage or not. It either helps you in your pursuit of wealth or it doesn't. Once you realize you live in a black and white world, each time you start to do whatever the bad habit is, you now have to consciously choose. Which do you value more? Do you value the relief of "busyness" or do you value growing your wealth?

People Buy You First

In order to be successful financially in most businesses, especially those where you have personal exposure to the public, you have to sell yourself first. If the prospect doesn't buy you, they won't buy your product or service. We all have habits that may not be serving our best interest. The good thing is that all habits, good or bad, are self-imposed, and they can be changed. To help you to recognize some habits that may cripple your chances at success and turn off your prospects, here are some specific things you may want to consider.

The habit doesn't accomplish anything at all. It only costs you time, energy, and money.

Maybe you have a habit of making personal calls during the time you have designated to make business calls, or you do non-business activities during the time you are supposed to be working at your business. With closer observation, you may discover that this habit is fueled by fear—a fear of being rejected by someone when you make a business call or a fear that your business may not succeed. So, you use personal calls as a smoke screen, a way of justifying to yourself that you are busy making calls or doing business activities. This could lead to a justification of why your business is not working. This habit is called "busyness" versus "business." What it is really called is hiding from the truth. And if you want success, you must look for truth (not hide from it), and then take action that leads you toward what you want.

The Habit Irritates Others.

Maybe you have the habit of always asking for compliments or standing right in someone's face when you speak. Maybe you clear your throat before each sentence. Maybe you tap your finger on the table or constantly insert a phrase like, "You know," or "Okay." Both relay to your prospect that you are not confident.

I remember when I first started speaking before large groups. One evening, I was speaking for two hours before about 200 people. I was nervous, but hoped it didn't show. At the end of my talk, I got a nice applause. I thought I had done pretty well. However, one woman walked up to me and said, "I really enjoyed some of the things you had to say, but I was distracted by the number of times you said 'okay.'"

I responded with, "I don't think I said 'okay' that many times."

She said, "I took the liberty of recording your talk, so if you want to listen for yourself, it might provide some valuable insight for you as you develop your speaking career."

She handed me the cassette tape. I put it in my pocket and thanked her, telling her I would listen to it. The next day, I laid the cassette on my desk. It laid there for over a month before I finally got up the courage to listen to it. As I listened, I started counting the amount of times I said 'okay' because I wanted to get back with her and let her know she was mistaken. I was shocked when I counted almost 200 times within a 2-hour talk! Almost every sentence ended with 'okay.' That was a life-changing moment for me. Later, I realized that the 'okay' was symbolic of a lack of confidence and my need for approval from the audience. You might want to observe yourself if you are using this habit. Notice what you're feeling at the time. You may discover a need for acceptance or a fear of rejection causing you to do it. Whatever the habit, if it's irritating to others, you can bet it is costing you business.

The Habit Makes You Look Foolish.

This doesn't mean you have to break every habit that someone else doesn't like, but you might want to just take a realistic look and ask yourself what habits you have that may be costing you business, credibility, etc. For example, I know someone who promotes a health product, yet she smokes about two packs of cigarettes a day. She does very well in her business, but my question is, how much better could she be doing if she got rid of a habit that causes her to lose credibility and look foolish? On a deeper level, if she really looked at her habit, she might discover that it is her need for attention that drives her smoking habit. Of course, we all know that it also becomes an addiction. But then again, seeking approval is also an addiction.

You Don't Approve of Your Own Habit.

It violates your own credibility, values and integrity in some way. Maybe you are always telling things that were told to you in confidence. No one knows except you, and it bothers you, but you do it anyway. Maybe you do it for recognition or to make it look like you know something that others don't; therefore you are more important. This can also be classified as a need for acceptance. Either way, you might find that it hurts your credibility without even knowing it.

Maybe you over state or over exaggerate your product in order to make a sale or entice someone to buy. You know you shouldn't, but you do it anyway. All I'm saying is, become more self-observant of how you may be coming across to others.

You get three primary payoffs for breaking bad habits. *One*, you get rid of something you didn't want or need in the first place. *Two*, you develop new insights into how you affect others. And *three,* it will greatly improve your chances at being successful.

I wish I could say that breaking unwanted habits without using any willpower is possible, but it isn't. You basically have to go "cold turkey." Just quit. You have to begin by making a fundamental choice not to engage in the habit.

So later, the two-pack-a-day woman came to me in a conversation told me she wanted to quit smoking. She said she had tried many different methods to quit and nothing worked.

I said to her, "You know it's affecting your health, as well as your business, right."

She said, "Yes, I know."

I said, "Did you know that the Surgeon General has said it will give you cancer? But you continue to do it anyway. Why?"

She said, "Yes, I know, and I don't know why I can't quit." She asked, "Can you help me?"

I said, "Yes I can help you, but you have to do some of the work." She agreed. I then asked what methods she had tried in the past to stop smoking. She named a few like the patch, gum, and a couple more. I ask her, "What are you doing right now to quit?"

She said, "I am trying the tapering method, where I still smoke, but taper off how many per day."

I responded back with, "It will do you absolutely no good to try to 'taper off.' It's like an alcoholic trying to taper off alcohol, or a heroin addict trying to taper off heroin. When you just taper off smoking, you still see yourself as a smoker. You can't be a smoker and a nonsmoker at the same time." I asked her, "Do you really truly want to quit?"

Her answer was a definite, "Yes!"

I said, "If you really want to quit, the very first thing you must do is make a fundamental choice, a decision, to be a non-smoker. Not to try to quit, but to be a non-smoker. You have to make a choice, a decision, to honor your own health more than the habit. The rest is easy once you begin to see yourself as a non-smoker." I asked her, "Can you make that decision now?"

She responded back with a definite, "YES!"

I said, "Okay, the next time you go to light up, I want you to remember your decision to be a non-smoker."

We took a break for lunch during the seminar. I watched as she finished her lunch, and out of habit, she walked outside the hotel onto the patio, took a pack of cigarettes out of her purse, and lit one up. She took one puff, stopped, looked at the cigarette, threw it on the ground, and stepped on it. Then, she walked to the trash can and tossed the pack. She told me later that she lit up out of habit, but when she took that puff, she said she couldn't stand the taste. Eight years later, she is still a non-smoker.

The same holds true for becoming wealthy. Once you really decide to be wealthy, then failure to do so is no longer an option. If you want wealth, you have to make a fundamental choice to *be* wealthy. You have to honor your success more than you do your present condition or the habits that keeps you stuck financially. Once you've made that choice, the rest is easy...success comes easily if you leave no room for failure.

Begin to observe your habits as they relate to your business, as well as your life, because they both interact. Do you say "yes" when you want to say "no?" Begin to notice what seems to bring out certain habits? Is it certain people you are with or certain situations that make you feel a certain way? The more you know and observe about your non-productive habits, the more you will be prepared to break them once and for all.

There are all kinds of habits. Some are good. Some are not so good. But the one thing they all have in common is they are voluntary and artificial, created and controlled by you. You create the *bad* and the *good*, and you can live without the bad ones. All it takes to change them is a firm decision to do so backed with some discipline.

Some habits can be good. In fact, you'd be lost without them. Some are just plain necessary in order to get on with living. You wouldn't want to change hands to brush your teeth, or learn to walk each time you got up to go across the room, would you? You probably have better things to do with your time. Good habits free your mind. You don't have to get up in the morning and wonder, "How do I get these pants on correctly?" Or get into your car and say, "Now, how do I drive this thing?" If you didn't have certain good habits, you'd be overwhelmed by the number of decisions you'd have to make to get the simplest things done. However, a habit is only as good as its premise. Most of us have habits that we don't like, habits that we would like to get rid of, habits that we've been meaning to break, 'one of these days.' If you want financial success faster, now's the time. Breaking a bad habit has its own reward, and then some. It will improve your business, your success, your finances, your life, and your personal growth overall.

Intention is the starting point for change. In order to make a permanent change, you must first set the intention to understand yourself. Self-knowledge is the beginning step toward success. Self-knowledge cannot be given to you by learning a system, or from someone else. You must discover it for yourself. If your intention to know yourself is weak, then just a casual wish or hope to change is of very little significance. Without knowing who you are, and what habits you need to change, there is no foundation for correct thinking; there is no reality. Without a foundation for correct thinking based upon self-knowledge, there can be no correct action. And without correct action, there can be no change. And without change there is no way to take your financial success to the next level.

Have you ever heard the statement, *"The truth will set you free?"* The truth begins with an understanding of, "That which we are without distortion." That's what the statement means. It's not referring to merely telling the truth, although that's a good place to start, but rather understanding or *seeing* the truth.

Knowing the truth about yourself is where the change that is necessary to go to the next level of financial success begins. It's called starting with what's real. Reality gives you true freedom. Reality comes from the understanding of *what is* without distortion. Whereas, when you're working toward reality through some system that someone else created for you to follow, or through motivation or positive thinking, or waiting for the "Law of Attraction" to bring it to you, that's called "postponement." That's called the cover up of *what is* with what you would like it to be. In order to create a new structure for your life, for your business success, your financial future, you must first truly want to be free of the bad habits that are costing you.

Of course, the worst bad habit of all I haven't yet mentioned. It's a disease and it's one that will absolutely destroy your chances at success in any endeavor. It's the disease known as procrastination! This is also a bad habit, one that can destroy your chances at success. Why do some fall into the procrastination trap time after time? Because procrastination becomes a way of coping with the emotions and physical symptoms that accompany fear. It may bring some temporary relief, but you eventually wake up the following day and find that no boy scouts have dropped in overnight and done your work for you. Most importantly, the next time you catch yourself saying, "I can do this later," think instead, "Just get it done!" Push on through the feelings and do it now. The feeling you get when you finish will be so much better than any relief you get from procrastinating.

Procrastinating: "I must get this job done right, or I'll be a total failure. There's just so much work to do. I'll wait until tomorrow when I am feeling better and can do a better job."

Reality: Not doing your work now will lead to a sloppy, rushed job just before your deadline and will leave you feeling too anxious to do a proper job.

Strategy: Look at why you are procrastinating. Does the thought of failing make you feel anxious? Take a few deep breaths, replace your negative thoughts and feelings of failure with thoughts and feelings of your previous successes.

SUCCESS AND WEALTH ARE LEARNED BEHAVIORS.

Twenty-three

Network to Increase Your Net-worth

"The world contains incredible diversity, but you cannot experience it all within the confines of your comfort zone."

--- Jim Britt

I've heard it said that communication is easy. I disagree. Talking is easy. Communication on the other hand—which is an exchange or communion with another—requires greater skill. A conversation you exchange with another, demands that you listen and speak skillfully, not just talk mindlessly. And when interacting with fear, anxiety, or frustration, communication can be even more difficult; we're much less skillful communicators when caught up in these types of emotions.

When it comes to building your network and wealth, effective communication is all about: first, receiving information that others are sending to you with as little distortion as possible, and second, conveying your messages to others clearly and effectively. In today's fast-paced world, most messages are muddled by busy, over-anxious senders, and oftentimes misinterpreted by the recipient because they have no clue what you are trying to convey. This can cause tremendous confusion, wasted effort, and missed opportunities to build your network of contacts.

You can't succeed alone. And it's not about working longer hours or working harder and setting more goals. It's about networking and connecting with the right individuals to accelerate your progress. Learn from those who have successfully done what you want to do.

Spend at least 15 minutes a day networking to increase your net worth. Whether it's online social networking, making phone calls, attending a luncheon or other networking function, all will add to your network and your net worth.

When meeting someone new, put their contact information immediately into your smart phone. Keep it organized and on hand, so you are ready for what comes next, whether it's friendship, a business alliance, or both. Nothing happens by accident and preparing for what's next assures that you are ready to move forward with the greatest likelihood of success.

I remember, years back, my wife and I were leaving a shopping mall. As we opened the door to exit, a business associate, James—whom I hadn't seen for many years—was entering. We stopped and chatted for a few minutes and before we parted, he asked for my business card. We said goodbye. As my wife and I walked away, I told her that I'd be getting a had written note from him within a few days. She said, "How do you know that?" I explained that, that was his method of operation to build and stay in touch with his network. Sure enough, three days later the note appeared in the mail.

Another experience was when I received a call from a friend and business connection, Carol. She presented classes in her home on creative visualization. She had a large room in her home that would seat about 40 people. She taught classes Monday through Thursday—a class in the afternoon, one in the evening, as well as a class on Saturday. Her classes were always full. One day, she called me in almost a panic explaining that her classes were empty, and she had no future reservations.

My first question was, "Are you practicing what you teach?" She assured me that she was, but no results. My next question was, "Where are you right now?"

She said, "I'm in my training room."

I asked, "Who else is in there with you?"

She said, "Just my bird."

I said, "Do you think the bird is going to buy?"

She said, "No, of course not."

So, my suggestion was to go where there are people. I said, "There is a breakfast club that meets on Thursday morning at the Hilton hotel with about 200 people attending." I said, "Go and tell the meeting organizer, Robert, that I sent you. It will cost you $5."

She asked, "What do I do when I get there?"

I said, "Register, say hello to Robert, have breakfast, and meet as many people as you can."

When she arrived, Robert was standing at the registration table and she introduced herself. Robert asked what type of business she was in. When she told him, he said, "I'd like to know more about what you do. I've always been interested in that sort of thing." They exchanged cards and she went in a sat down.

The keynote speaker got up to make her presentation. She was using a slide projector (for the millennial's that was our first PowerPoint.) About a minute into her presentation, the bulb blew out in her projector. However, she had a spare, which she promptly installed and resumed. About another two minutes and the second bulb blew. She said, "I'm sorry, but I can't present without my projector." Robert immediately turned to Carol and asked if she could make a presentation regarding her topic, and that he thought the audience would be interested.

Of course, Carol said, "Yes."

Guess what happened? Right. She filled up two classes with almost 40 people in each.

Later, she called all excited. She said, "I couldn't believe the woman's bulb blew twice, and then he asked me, a first-time attendee to make a presentation." She said, "It was all amazing."

I said, "Carol, you blew the two bulbs with your intention and the value you were going to bring to the group."

Network to increase your net-worth! You never know whom you might meet. When encountering a challenge, like Carol was experiencing, try not to convince yourself that it is not meant to be; it's just not meant to be easy. You gotta think! If you want success in any area of your life, you have to get off the couch and go for it! Because nothing happens without taking action.

And when you network, how you communicate is of utmost importance. If you attend a meet up, don't think, 'I am here to make money or get new clients.' Instead think, 'I am here to help others.'

Keep this in mind; Communication is only successful when both the sender and the receiver understand the same information. Oftentimes, ideas that you actually send do not necessarily reflect what you want to get across, causing a communications breakdown and creating roadblocks that could stand in the way of your relationships, networking, and business building opportunities. This can especially happen with text and email correspondence—especially with auto correct.

Funny story. A friend was closing a really big deal, and he and his client were texting back and forth. He texted, "I'll take care of it." His auto-correct took over and texted, "I love you."

He frantically called the client to explain it was auto-correct.

Being able to communicate effectively is essential if you want to build a successful network of top-quality people. To do this, you must understand what your message is, who you are sending it to, and how it will be perceived. You must also weigh-in the circumstances surrounding. If, for example, you are trying to get your business across to someone on an elevator ride between a couple floors, you are very likely going to communicate your message ineffectively.

So, what's the secret to learning how to communicate effectively?

Making a Great First Impression is a good place to start. It takes just a quick glance, a few seconds, for someone to evaluate you when you meet for the first time. In this short time, the other person forms an opinion about you based on your appearance, your body language, your demeanor, your mannerisms, and how confident you are. Think about it. You see a person for the first time and right away you get an initial "feel" for the person. They have a smile and seem friendly. They are well dressed and look professional. They walk with confidence. They look you in the eye. They have a firm handshake. And they seem pleasant when they start to speak. All these things are part of the communication process, and especially the first impression. With every new encounter, you are evaluated and the person's impression of you is formed. These first impressions can be nearly impossible to reverse or undo, making those first encounters extremely important, for they set the tone for the relationships.

Be yourself and be at ease. It doesn't mean that you have to do all the talking. If you are feeling uncomfortable and on edge, and talk too much to compensate, this can make the other person ill at ease and that's a sure way to create the wrong first impression. If you are calm and confident, the other person will feel more at ease. When you are trying too hard to win the approval of another, they feel your energy, your intention. On the other hand, be careful not to come off too confident so that it feels too much like you are trying to control the conversation. Just remember that people are people and most everyone will respond favorably to you when you are friendly and relaxed and not trying to be someone you're not.

Remember this: People are looking for reasons to listen and form a relationship, just as people are looking for reasons not to listen and not form relationships. To communicate effectively, ask questions and listen. Maybe you can help them solve a problem. What do they need, what problems do they have, and how can you help to solve that problem? Maybe you can offer them a referral. Maybe you can or maybe you can't. Either way, people like to talk about themselves, and if you listen with interest, they will return the dialog with similar questions back to you.

Here's a great rule for communication I learned from experience. If it is not necessary to say, then it is necessary not to say. Think about that statement for a moment. If it is not necessary to say, then it is necessary not to say. It simply means to leave out the stuff that has no benefit to the person with which you are communicating. Barriers to building your business almost always stem from offering too much information too fast or information that has no meaning for the receiver. For example, the greatest mistake made is "dumping the whole load" before establishing a need or interest. When in doubt, just remember that less is more.

Get good at asking questions and establishing a need. One of the quickest routes to an awkward silence is by asking questions that can be simply answered with yes or no. For example, you might ask a stranger you just met in the ski lodge, "Do you ski?" Their response is, "Yes." Where do you go from there? Or you could ask the question, "How do you like skiing here?" By asking a question that requires a more detailed answer, the other person has to elaborate and offer as much information as possible. Why ask, "Are you enjoying yourself?" when the question could be phrased, "What do you think of this party?" That can start the communication process off in the right direction.

I refer to asking the right questions as, "The Art of Networking and Effective Communication." Let's say for example, that you are an affiliate selling nutritional supplements. You just met a woman at Starbucks and strike up a conversation. When you ask her questions, ones that make her think and feel, the answers you receive will be the signs that carry you to your first three destinations.

Your first destination is, "Do they have a problem or pain?"

Your second destination is, "Do they want to solve it?"

Your third destination is, "Can you help them solve it?"

Those are the first three things you want to discover to determine if you have a viable prospect. In other words, instead of focusing on making the sale, focus on whether there is a sale to be made in the first place. The same holds true for any type of product or business. You are there to solve problems.

When you listen to your prospect, the correct approach will materialize before you. For example, let's say you provide people with an opportunity to work from home. So, if you hear a single mom saying that she is stressed out because she has to leave her children every day, and therefore can't give them the quality time they need. Of course, an obvious benefit would be, you could offer her an opportunity to work from home. However, before offering her the opportunity, build some history.

Here's what I mean:

- Ask what her present work is.
- Ask if she likes her job.
- Ask if she has to commute to work every day.
- Ask if she feels she is getting paid what she is worth.
- Ask what an ideal job would be.
- If she says that she would like to work from home, then ask what she would like to do?

The answers to your questions will help her discover and reinforce her real desire to work from home. Remember, she will always have the answers to what she wants, but she will probably not have a solution. That is your job once you have arrived at your first destination—establishing a need.

Questions force them to talk and gives you information. It helps you uncover problems and discover if there is a real need, a problem, or a pain. Questions help you understand her priorities. What is important to her? You might say that questions help you diagnose the problem or pain. Questions also help you establish your own credibility, which should be to help the prospect find a solution to their problem. Questions make your prospect feel that you want to play a key role in helping them find a solution. Their answers help you paint the right picture in the mind of your prospect. Pictures that are benefit oriented. You get to create the picture yourself based on the questions you ask and listening to her responses. But more importantly, your prospect gets to see it in their mind and discover that they in fact do have a problem.

Questions will help you to break the ice. By asking a simple question like, "How are you today?" you can get a response or an opening that leads to the next question and the process of discovery. Questions allow you to plant your own ideas at the appropriate time. "What if you took this approach? What if you started your own business working from home? Have you ever thought of that?"

Questions let you handle their concerns in the form of an answer during the course of the conversation, instead of as an objection that needs to be overcome. Questions put you in control, not for manipulation purposes, but for the purpose of keeping the conversation on track. Use the power of asking questions, instead of telling people what you know or making statements. Learn to ask questions that will help you discover what they know about the subject first. Don't make a statement until you know they have a need. If you feed someone a solution before asking questions and arriving at your first destination, you may become the one that owns the problem and the solution, which will take you nowhere.

If you simply tell someone that your business opportunity will provide them with financial freedom, the conversation will probably stop there, because you have not yet established a need. On the other hand, if you ask them if working from home is important to them, you can start a conversation that leads to other questions that will establish whether they have a need or not and whether they want to solve it.

The key to mastering the art of networking is to master the art of asking questions—and listening—in order to arrive at your first three destinations. Do they have a problem? Do they want to solve it? Can you solve it?

Be careful not to rattle off a string of questions too fast or try to propose marriage on the first encounter. A conversation should not be an interrogation or make someone feel uncomfortable.

Another interesting point that Golub makes has to do with self-worth.

He says that self-worth is synonymous with confidence and regardless of rejection, a person's self worth does not change. All too often, people are afraid to take a chance because they fear rejection. Rejection makes a person feel inferior. In reality, rejection does not change one's self-worth. You are still the same person, as valuable and important as you were before you entered the conversation.

No one can take your self-worth away from you; only you can do that. Rejection is an illusion until it actually happens. Why spend time worrying about a "what if" situation? Take a chance and keep trying for what you want. It's only a matter of time before you get it. The only way to learn how to communicate with people and to hone your skills is by practicing. Hanging back in the shadows and playing it safe leads nowhere.

Start Small

Learning how to communicate with people takes time to develop and everyone will advance at their own pace. Start small; become comfortable with each of these steps one at a time. At its foundation, effective communication starts with confidence and this is the thread that binds everything else together. Each encounter helps to increase your confidence and diversify your experiences. A good place to practice these new people skills is the office or in the store. After it has become easier to speak with peers, try talking to people in higher positions of power, such as managers. In no time, the skills you taught yourself regarding how to communicate with people will become second nature and won't require any thought at all. Talking to someone like the CEO of a major company will be a breeze.

Nobody ever said learning how to communicate with people would be easy. For some, mustering the confidence required will be a huge step. This is probably the most difficult part, but once you take that step, the rest will fall into place. Have faith in yourself and know that you are as worthy as the next person. Effective communication is an important skill everyone should know, as it is the key to future success and advancement in practically every aspect of life.

Test Your Social Skills IQ

Communication is the key to social skills, but when communication breaks down, social ineptitude takes on a life of its own. As children we were taught that it's not OK to blurt out derogatory names just because someone has upset us. We're not supposed to throw tamper tantrums when we can't have what we want, that sharing is smiled upon, while pushing and shoving to be first in line is not. Find out just how savvy you are with this social skills quiz.

Rate This Article:

When you ask questions, really take an active interest in what this person is saying, and if it is a subject you know nothing about, you can use it to your advantage. Even admit that it is not a familiar topic. Would she mind telling you more about it? People love to share what they know, and nothing increases confidence more than sharing a subject close to the heart.

Example: You meet someone at the cocktail lounge in a hotel and you get into a conversation.

"Where are you from?"

"I live in Halifax, Nova Scotia."

"Really. I've never been there. What's it like?" Now, you are in a conversation. You can keep asking questions. "What's the weather like? What's the population? What do you do for a living?" which will start a whole new conversation.

Listening is one of the most important skills you can develop in building your network. How well you listen has a major impact on the quality of your relationship with others. Relationships are the lifeblood of a business and your wealth building.

Why do you want to listen?

Listen to obtain information.

Listen to understand.

Listen for enjoyment.

Listen to learn.

Listen to establish a need.

Listen to help solve a problem.

Listen so you know what to say and how to say it when it's your turn to speak.

The fact is that most people are not good at listening at all. Clearly, listening is a skill that we can all benefit from improving. By becoming a better listener, you will improve your confidence and productivity, as well as your ability to influence and persuade. The way to become a better listener is to practice active listening. This is where you make a conscious effort to hear not only the words that another person is saying, but more importantly, to try and understand the total message being sent. It takes a lot of concentration and determination to be an active listener. Old habits are hard to break, and if your listening habits are as bad as many peoples are, then there's a lot of habit-breaking to do! Just be deliberate with your listening and remind yourself constantly that your goal is to truly hear what the other person is saying. Set aside all other thoughts and behaviors and concentrate on the message.

Learn to start conversations. All too often, people are afraid to take a chance and be the first to start a conversation because they fear rejection. Rejection makes a person feel inferior. In reality, rejection is about one's self-worth. It's not about the other person at all. Place no person above you. Here's the key. No one can take your self-worth away from you; only you can do that. No one can reject you unless you give them permission to do so. Rejection is an illusion. You may think that you are being rejected when in reality the other person is just having a bad day or is thinking about something else. Why spend time worrying about a "what if" situation? Take a chance and keep going for what you want. The only way to learn how to communicate with people and hone your skills is by practicing. Hanging back in the shadows and playing it safe will lead you nowhere.

Each encounter helps to increase your confidence and diversify your experiences and network. The more experiences you have communicating with others, the better you become at it. Try talking with strangers in the supermarket. Better yet, just ask them a question and see how long you can keep them talking. I called a wrong number on purpose one time to see how long I could keep them on the phone. Seven minutes! In no time, the skills you teach yourself around how to communicate with people will become second nature and won't require any thought at all. Eventually, it will become a breeze.

NO ONE CAN TAKE YOUR SELF-WORTH AWAY FROM YOU; ONLY YOU CAN DO THAT.

Twenty-four

Your Legacy Lives On

"Observe this moment…you are creating your future and legacy."

--- Jim Britt

Of all the things in your life which fall under the category of non-negotiable, this is one which you will want to gain clarity on and give 100% commitment to as quickly as possible.

What is it? Your legacy. Like it or not we will all leave a legacy. The question is not whether you'll leave a legacy, but what legacy you will leave. Your legacy is much too important to be left to chance. And that is why thinking intentionally about your life's existence, experiences, and contribution to others is one of the most important things any of us has to do.

What I'm saying is, begin thinking more deeply about your life, your purpose, the examples you set, and what your life represents.

What do I want to do with my life?

Why am I here?

What example am I setting for my family and future generations?

How can I contribute?

What will I leave behind?

By defining your legacy, most decisions will be made for you in advance. You will know what actions to take to lead you in that direction. You will also avoid conflict between what you want and how you go about attaining it.

One of the tremendous benefits of deciding your legacy is that it will bring a level of clarity into your daily activities like never before. Knowing your legacy will impress upon you the necessity of clearly defined objectives, fulfillment of your responsibilities, honoring your intentions, and following through on your commitments.

Look at your legacy as a sort of symbolic immortality. In other words, take an in-depth look and consider the impact of your legacy and how it will impact the next five generations. Yes, five generations! Your life is actually a gift to future generations. The example you set, the legacy you leave, will continue in some way to participate in the lives of others long after you are gone. The question is what will that participation be? Rather than focusing on leaving an inheritance, let your character, your values, and the example of a life well-lived be your family heirloom to future generations.

Look at it this way. Your legacy is like a self-portrait. It is the signature of your life's presence. So why not make this life of yours into a work of art. We only live once, but once is enough if you do it right. Your legacy lives on.

By building your life on a foundation of style, class, and dignity, you place an exclamation, rather than a question mark, after it. So, why not mark today as the day you decide to focus on your legacy. Focus on the specific things you can do to make a significant and lasting contribution to future generations. When you take your final bow, how will you be remembered?

WILL YOU BE JUST A FOOTNOTE IN HISTORY OR A HEADLINE?

Twenty-five

Mastering the Art of Leadership

"True leadership is the art of inspiring others to action through one's own exemplary behavior."

--- Jim Britt

If you thought you could truly make a difference, would you be willing to step out of the crowd and be all that you can be? If you discovered that you possessed untapped leadership qualities and skills, would you use them? If you knew that you could inspire others to make a difference, would you be compelled to do so?

No matter what your role may be, you can choose to become a more powerful, effective leader. With a few simple, yet powerful, tools you can develop your leadership skills and use them to influence and inspire others.

Right now, there are men and women just like you, from every walk of life, from all sorts of businesses and from every social and economic level, making a difference because they, like you, care deeply about something. They are using their leadership skills to make a difference. They are different themselves. What sets them apart from the masses? It's not their level of education. It's not how much money they earn. It's not where they come from, who they know. It's not their sex, age, or occupation. It's their awareness and sensitivity to the needs of others, awareness of the challenges others face. It is their enthusiasm for improving things and for creating new opportunities. They have a passion for a cause bigger than themselves, and they have a deep desire to give something back to society. In looking for new ways of making a difference and serving others, they have tapped into their personal power and leadership potential.

There are common qualities that effective leaders possess. These qualities are characteristics present in all of us to some degree. To develop them and put them to use, you are not required to study complex theories or employ psychological gymnastics. Simple common-sense ideas and attitudes that individually and collectively make you a more dynamic, effective leader is the key. Some of these qualities are "how to" skills and some are people skills. Others may involve philosophies and attitudes.

Leadership is not something you learn once and for all. It is an ever-evolving set of skills, ideas and talents that will evolve and change as you do. To become an effective leader, you must first have a clear definition of what these leadership qualities are, a mission as well as an honest desire to improve yourself and make a difference to others.

Effective leaders, inspire others to aim higher, work harder and smarter, accomplish more in less time, and enjoy doing it. Every coach has a game plan. Every military officer has a battle plan

Every airline pilot has a flight plan. And every leader in pursuit of wealth should have a system for bringing out the best in others.

When you or your business wind up in the winner's circle, you can rest assured it wasn't by accident. It was because you and your team collectively did their job. And you, as the company leader, did your job very well.

You inspired your team with a vision of success.

You were sensitive to every individual's needs.

You challenged your team members to stay focused and on purpose.

You encouraged and supported your team when they were down.

You kept your team motivated and with a desire to be winners.

You became a mentor for your team, setting the example and sharing your insight and experiences.

You provided the common vision and goal that held the team together.

You inspired your team to give their best despite the odds.

You were the confident leader who encouraged your team to take initiative and teach others how to make contributions that benefited the organization as a whole.

All these things are principles followed by effective leaders in order to get into and remain in the winner's circle.

What is leadership? Leadership simply means this: "The courage to be first." Leadership is not a position. Just like in any game, without a coach or leader, the player wouldn't know how to score, which direction to run, and maybe not even know how to play the game at all. Everyone needs a coach, someone to teach them the rules of the game. Otherwise, a person might spend all their time on the defensive, not knowing that the only way to win is to play the offensive. What if a team member didn't know the rules and didn't have a leader? Could they possibly run in the wrong direction? Everyone needs a coach, a leader.

How do you become an effective leader, whether in business, your community, or family?

An effective leader sets the example. As a leader, we live under a microscope. Nothing we do or say escapes the scrutiny and examination of our followers. This is one of the most important secrets of effective leadership. As a leader, our followers mirror the example we set for them. In a family you see it all the time. As they are growing up, children look to their parents for guidance. If they don't get it from their parents, they look to their peers and ever join a gang to find someone to look up to for guidance.

As a leader, we must ask ourselves repeatedly, "What message am I sending? What example am I setting? What environment am I creating?" When you, as a leader, set out to make a difference, your beliefs, words, and actions inspire others to follow. As a leader, setting the example comes first and foremost. In short, you are accountable. If a leader doesn't return phone calls, for example, they are teaching their team members not to follow up. An effective leader must talk-the-talk and walk-the-walk if they want others to do the same.

An effective leader must be willing to serve. Service has a high value. If you contribute your time, energy, emotions, and effort, you will have a real impact on people and their problems. When you make a contribution to the well-being and performance of others, your level of fulfillment and success will be immeasurable. Service is an attitude, not a department. Everyone within an organization should be responsible for service, especially the person at the top. How deep your service runs, and the type, kind, and quality of service given, will be a major key to the success of an organization. Effective leaders know that service starts at the top. It starts with one person. A leader's slogan should be, "Service starts here."

An effective leader takes full responsibility for everything! A leader's job is influencing human behavior, regardless of the goal. They never point toward someone else or an outside circumstance as the cause of their problems. They take full responsibility for their own actions, the actions of their team members, as well as the end result produced. Responsibility is defined as "the ability to respond" or "response-ability." A good leader takes full responsibility for how they feel, their own actions, and their results. They take full responsibility for how their team members feel and how they perform.

A good leader also knows that team building is like a farmer planting a crop. The farmer plants seeds. They are all unique. Some grow and some don't. It's called the Law of Averages. If the farmer wants to increase his averages and his yield, he simply increases the nourishment; that's always a fine balance. With his crops, the farmer can provide too much or too little. Either one can destroy the crop. Same with people; you can give too much or too little nourishment. A fine balance is the key.

It's your job as a leader to nourish your team and keep the weeds out. You have to be quick with the hoe, to cut the weeds of fear, doubt, rejection, and other types of negativity that will smother your harvest. At the same time, the effective leader must not over nourish his or her team members. A leader must take full responsibility for the growth and yield of his or her team, whether they have one or five hundred on their team—or in their family.

An effective leader must have a vision. Vision is defined as, "seeing with your imagination." As a leader, it is important to clearly know where you are going, and even more importantly, why. Why do you want what you want? What compels you to do what you do? You will know that answer when you find the true purpose that drives you, the pure "essence" of why you want what you want. Your vision can be small or earth-shaking, but the most important part is that it be clear. Clarity is knowing both what you want to accomplish and why you want to accomplish it. A leader's vision, whether clear of fuzzy, will have an effect on those around them.

Your commitment to your vision becomes an example of leadership that will inspire and motivate others to have their own version of a mission within your mission. Whatever your vision, it is a powerful and magnetic leadership quality. Vision makes leaders stand out in a crowd. Vision is at the heart of effective leadership.

An effective leader sells everything—always! Every event, every lunch meeting, every training, every call, every meeting is a special event! An effective event is a sold event! If an event is worth having, it is worth selling. What I am saying is, as a leader, you must make sure you give everything value! Your team members will receive what they "believe" they're receiving, and you can only sell an event, a new company policy, a new selling tool, or anything else to the degree that you believe in its value.

So, what is an event? It is everything that's good about your business. A convention, or national meeting, a company beach party, a planning session with your team, a training, a special sales conference call, a special awards dinner, a sales contest, etc. are all special events. They are events worth selling. If they are worth having, they should be worth selling their value. A good leader creates value for everything! Learn to make everything a special event!

An effective leader makes others feel special. I remember talking to an accountant at a meeting once. I asked if he was going to be attending my training the following Saturday. He said he wasn't, that that was the day he had set aside to do his taxes.

The first thing I did was to make my training on Saturday more valuable to him than preparing his taxes. In other words, I sold the event. I created value. I sold the event as the only place to be that Saturday, and the most important event in the 20th century.

My next objective was to make him feel special at the same time, so we talked in length about what he wanted in life and how to go about accomplishing his dreams. He had my undivided attention, and all we talked about was how to help him have more in his life. That conversation made him feel special.

Here's the note he sent me about a week following the training he attended.

"Thanks Jim, for taking the time with me at the meeting and convincing me to attend the training on Saturday. It made me feel really special. Just like you promised, it was the best training I've ever attended. My sales have already increased in a big way as a result of it, just like you said they would.

Thank you so much!"

Bill

Creating value for others and making them feel special are two effective leadership traits that just can't be overlooked.

An effective leader is sensitive. Sensitive leadership is not leadership that lacks strength or courage. It does not lessen a leader's power as some might think. A sensitive leader has a heightened awareness of issues, values and the people within his/her organization. Sensitive leadership simply means having the ability to stay focused on the world in which they operate, and in particular, on the people they lead. Sensitivity doesn't distract from other leadership qualities. It adds to them. For example, decision making requires a greater sensitivity because the business world can change so rapidly. That also makes business risky, and risk requires being sensitive to all the elements of those risks, including the potential outcome for all involved.

Risk taking is a major part of leadership. When you consider successful leaders who make a difference, we see that they have the courage to take action while others are waiting for a better time, a safer situation, or assured results. Effective leaders are willing to take risks because they know that being too cautious and indecisive kills opportunity.

A leader should be sensitive to others needs and take every opportunity to appreciate the efforts of those on their team. There is always something to appreciate in every individual. You don't have to wait for record breaking sales months. A good leader looks for ways to recognize and appreciate others. They are sensitive to the little things that make a big difference in the lives of others.

A sensitive leader is a good listener. If someone has something bothering them, they know that if they don't listen, if that person has doubt, for example, that doubt creates uncertainty and uncertainty puts that person "out of productiveness." In other words, they are stuck until the issue gets resolved.

An effective Leader always keeps their team members connected. The greatest of all human needs is the need to feel connected. A heart connection is what I call the nutrients of the soul. People in organizations all over the world are dying every day from malnutrition. They are dying because they have lost that sense of connection.

What do you connect people to? First, you connect them to you, their leader. The more you do toward helping others attain their dreams, the more they feel connected and loyal to you. Through direct and indirect communications, you connect them to their goals and dreams. Learning to paint vivid pictures of their future, and place them into the picture, is a trait that every leader must develop. Remember, when you are painting pictures, it should be a picture of what they want for themselves, not what you want for them. People work for their reasons, not yours. A company and its leaders accomplish their goals by helping others within the organization accomplish their goals and dreams.

Keep them connected to the product or service they are selling, its quality and it benefits others.

Keep them connected to the team. A team can become like a second family. People love being part of a team.

Keep them connected to the company. Help them see the company as their partner in business. Connect them to the company and its leaders at every opportunity.

Keep them connected to a cause. The cause is not making money as some believe. There's no loyalty to money. Find the bigger cause, then keep them connected to it.

Every time you see a team member is an opportunity to reconnect. Always be asking yourself, "How can I reconnect with this person?"

If all your team members felt connected in every way, how would they feel? How would they perform? How dedicated would they be? How would you feel?

An effective leader guides their team on three primary levels. First, by helping each member of his team discover and eliminate underlying blocks that restrict them from performing at their full potential. Next, by igniting inspiration, leaving team members with a clear sense of direction that leads toward future growth and increased productivity. Third, working with each person on your team to duplicate the process in them, thereby building depth and strength within the organization as a whole.

A great leader studies human nature on three levels:

Great Leaders Study Possibility. What *could* exist? Leaders understand that there is always something more they could do to benefit the team as a whole. They look for ways to assist each member's personal growth. They make a study of what is possible. They are constantly playing the "what if" game with themselves as well as each member of the team.

Great Leaders Study Opportunity. They know that every encounter presents an opportunity to make a connection, to further develop a relationship, and to increase their network. They are always looking for ways to connect, to better themselves, and to improve performance. They know that every connection they make, every meeting they conduct, every email they send out, and every telephone call they make represents an opportunity to further develop relationships and improve performance.

Great Leaders Study Inevitability. If you were to start driving your car on Interstate 10 in Jacksonville, Florida, and headed west, where would you end up if you didn't stop? You would inevitability run off the end of the Santa Monica Peer in Southern California, or thereabouts. That's called inevitability.

A great leader watches herself/himself, the company, the direction he or she and each member of the team is headed and knows inevitability where they are going to end up on their present course. He or she also knows when it's necessary to make course corrections and helps team members to see those corrections as necessary.

There's a story about an egotistical captain of a battleship. One night, he was navigating in heavy fog. It was almost impossible to see. Suddenly, he saw a blinking light dead ahead. He radioed ahead with a message, "We are on a collision course, change course 30 degrees to the left."

A message came right back, "You change your course 30 degrees to the right."

Feeling a little put out, he radioed again, "I am a Captain, change your course 30 degrees to the left."

The message came back, "I am also a Captain, change your course 30 degrees to the right."

Getting really angry, he radioed back, "I am a battleship, and I suggest you change your course 30 degrees to the left!"

The message came back, "I am a Light House, and I suggest you change your course 30 degrees to the right."

As you move forward you will most certainly encounter obstacles. A good leader looks ahead and knows what they are dealing with, then takes immediate, appropriate action to solve the problem with the least amount of conflict.

Also, know that strength cannot exist without resistance. You can't build muscle if you don't lift the weights. A good leader always looks for the point of strength in every obstacle he or she may encounter. A good leader knows that the limit of their current view does not represent his or her capacity to create a solution to a problem.

So, as you go about your business this week, ask yourself these questions:

What is possible?

If I truly applied myself in every way what could I accomplish?

What opportunities are available to me?

What opportunities am I passing up that I could take advantage of?

THE MOST IMPORTANT QUESTION YOU SHOULD BE ASKING YOURSELF DAILY IS, ON MY PRESENT COURSE, WHERE WILL I INEVITABLY END UP?

Twenty-six

Core values

"You already possess the qualities you wish you had."

--- Jim Britt

What are core values and why is it important to know what they are?

Let's first start with core beliefs. These are the fundamental beliefs of a person. Beliefs do not necessarily represent your core values. However, the core beliefs you have are what dictate behavior, action, and results. For example, based on your upbringing, you could have a core belief that money is hard to earn, rich people are dishonest, money is the root of all evil, and so on. And now as an adult, you find yourself barely making ends meet financially.

Your core beliefs actually shape your personal reality before you are even aware of experiencing that reality. They make many of your decisions for you, right or wrong. Core beliefs are like sunglasses that filter the light before you perceive it. Just like your beliefs filter the outcomes in your life. You may want one thing but as you filter it through your belief system it changes, and you get something totally different. If you filter getting wealthy through a belief that, "Money is difficult to earn," you definitely won't get wealth.

The statement, "I'll believe it when I see it," is actually backward. We see and experience things because we believe them. In other words, your core beliefs filter how you view the world and what shows up in your view that you pay attention to. Two people see the same thing but perceive it differently because they are filtering it through different core beliefs. Your personal levels of reality are the result of observing what is around you and choosing what to accept or not accept based on your core beliefs. We automatically reject what is not compatible with our core beliefs.

I've heard people say something like, "I want to make a million dollars," yet they don't believe they can. They may have a core belief that money is hard to earn, only for the lucky few, or for those already rich. They may then defend that belief by putting down those who have money, saying money is not important, blaming the outside world or the government, or justifying why the average person can never be rich. They will make sure they can justify believing what they believe in some way. They don't think it through and contemplate the outcomes because all this happens in an instant, like looking up a key word on Google. Which ones do you pay attention to? For the most part, the ones on the first page. Same thing happens in your brain when you decide to become wealthy. Up pops your top ten reasons why you can never be rich. And it happens in a split second before you have time to consider whether the information is real or past subconscious programming.

You've heard me say before that all beliefs are false. A belief is something we have decided is true, but it may not be true at all. It is only true for you based on your programming; some beliefs were programmed consciously and some unconsciously, but all were programmed just the same. We all have beliefs, and we all have beliefs that we'd like to change. Am I correct?

So, let's look at how we might go about changing some of those unwanted beliefs. Let's start with your core values.

Unlike beliefs, which you have been programmed to believe, core values can help you know the difference between what's right or wrong for you, and what needs changing. Core values can help you determine whether you are on the right path toward fulfilling your life's purpose. The fact is, core values create an unwavering and unchanging guide from which to live your life. Think of core beliefs as points of power that resonate with you so intently you just *know* they are right for you. They inspire you. You feel passionate about them. You feel passionate and feel that tingling in your gut when you think about them. Your core values are basically the guidelines for your life.

To tell you the truth, at an early age, I never thought about core values. Most of us don't.

Not only did I not know what my core values were, but I had no idea that it was important for me to find out either. It wasn't until I got involved with personal development that I started to look at my core values.

So, why is it so important that you know your core values? Because your core tell you what's most important for you in life and lead you toward developing a core belief that supports it or changing beliefs that do not support it.

Basically, whether you know your core values or not, they are the very things that make you act and react in life the way you do. When you go against a core value, you feel the inner conflict. Let's say you say, "yes" to something out of the need for approval, when in reality you wanted to say, 'no." You feel the tug in your gut telling you that you should not say, "yes" when you wanted to say, "no." If you say, "yes," it will strengthen your belief that you need approval from another. You say, "no," you are honoring your core value of saying what you want without needing anyone's approval. You are giving your life to a new core belief and letting that need for approval wither away from lack of attention.

When you know your core values, what's most important to you in life, many of your decisions are made for you in advance. For example, if you have a core value of honesty, and you are faced with a situation that is not honest, your answer is automatically, "No, I don't do that." If one of your core values is integrity and someone asks you to do something that jeopardizes your integrity you say, "Thanks, but that doesn't work for me." You don't have to think about, or wrestle with a decision, your decision is made based on your core values.

Here's an important key. When your lifestyle matches your core values, you're happy.

When your lifestyle goes against your core values, you're not happy. Also, when your core values conflict with one another, you're not happy either.

Knowing your core values will help you know and pursue what's important to you in life and be firm about it. Knowing your core values will help you recognize and to let go of those core beliefs that no longer serve your greater good. Knowing your core values will help you with indecision and procrastination as well. In other words, when you know what your core values are, you don't waste valuable time working on things or putting things off that do not support your core values in the first place.

Keep in mind that core values are not set in stone, they may change over the course of your life. For example, a forty-year-old may not have the same core values as he or she did at 20. Look back at your life and you'll see what I mean.

You could have a long list of core values as well. Here are some examples:

Always striving to be your best

Keeping your commitments

Personal freedom

Taking care of your health

Exercise

Being on time

Loyalty

Adventure

Professionalism

Reliability

Self-control

Trustworthiness

Honesty

Truthfulness

Your list could contain dozens more. Make a list as long as you can, then pick the 10 core values that you most relate to. If you don't want to take the time now to make the list, just take a moment and think of the ten top qualities that fit you best. Then, look at your list and see if your 3 to 5 most important core values happen to conflict with one another; you may be facing some challenges in your life that you might not have been able to put your finger on until now.

Here's what happens when values conflict. Let's say that your 5 main values are freedom, success, security, adventure and family. You could have a conflict there.

While freedom, success, and adventure might go well together, security and family might tie you down a little. Now, you have a possible conflict. Doesn't mean you do, just that a potential conflict may exist that you may need to address.

Here's what I mean. On one hand you want to be adventurous, which will expose you to challenges and possibly taking risks. While on the other hand you want security and family that will make you refrain from taking such risks and challenges. See what I mean? When you were younger, mountain climbing was exciting and adventurous, and you thrived on the risk. But now you have a family to support and be there for, so your core values may have to change.

Another conflicting value situation would be if your main core values are freedom and success, and you feel trapped in an underpaid job. If you find yourself in such a situation, you will find it very hard to continue this way and be happy with your life at the same time. I've seen this value conflict thousands of times with participants in my seminars. Your body will be in one place while your heart and soul will want to go the opposite way, which leaves you feeling empty and frustrated inside. If this is you, it may be time to consider re-inventing yourself and your core values.

These mixed value combinations can create inner conflict, leading to stress and anxiety and can affect every area of your life, health, family, finances, etc. The reason is, you feel stuck someplace you don't want to be, while wanting something more and different at the same time. However, this doesn't mean you have to make an abrupt change. Just take small steps in the right direction based on your values. If you want out of a job but can't afford to quit, you may want to look at starting a part time business on the side. These are just examples, but I'm sure you see what I mean! You are going to have to figure out what's most important to you, by asking yourself what truly makes you the happiest, more complete, fulfilled, and what brings you the most satisfaction.

Core values are traits or qualities that you consider not just worthwhile, but that represent your highest priorities in life. They are core, fundamental driving forces that direct your life. Core values are called "guiding principles" because they form a solid core of who you are at a cellular level. Core values form the foundation for everything that happens in your life.

The importance of clearly defining your core values has multiple benefits. First of all, it gives your life purpose. When you haven't clearly defined your core values, you basically just end up drifting along in life with no direction or purpose. You get excited, motivated, set goals, but without your core values directing you, nothing much happens—just drifting, hoping someday something will change. Without core values, instead of basing your decisions and goals on your internal guidelines, you end up making decisions and setting goals based on social pressure, circumstances, or past programming. You end up trying to fulfill other people's expectations instead of your own. And then before you know it, your life has passed you by and you haven't even started to live. Without established core values, at the end of your life, you could look back and realize you've only lived 10% of what you could have lived. Trying to be someone else, following someone else's values, or living without your own core values is downright exhausting and will leave you feeling empty. On the other hand, living your life in line with your core values gives you a sense of purpose and direction.

Defining your core values will help you make the right choices. Otherwise, you could end up making choices and taking actions that actually conflict with your values. And when your actions conflict with your core values, the end result can be frustration, stress, depression, lack, and living an unhappy life.

Defining your core values will also increase your level of confidence. When you take the time to truly think through what you value most, and write those things down, you'll find it will increase your level of confidence, giving you more courage to make the right choices based on those values. The more you think about, and apply your core values, the more courage and confidence you develop and the more committed you will become to living them.

Defining your core values just makes life simpler. Why? Because when you know your core values, decision making becomes almost automatic. The reason is, when you are faced with a decision, you simply ask yourself, "Does this decision or action align with my core values?" If it does, you do it. If not, you don't. That simple! Instead of wrestling with what to do and what decision to make, or wasting your valuable time, you simply let your internal compass, your core values, guide you.

Here's a good exercise that will help you define your core values. Start by writing down as many of your core values as possible. Your list could contain a hundred or more.

Once you have a long list, prioritize and pick your top ten. Then, each day for 10 days compare each one on your top ten list to the longer list. So, let's say that you have 100 items and a top ten. Each day take one of your top ten and compare it to each of your 100 items individually.

Let's say you have these on your list of 100:

Keeping your commitments

Taking care of your health

Exercise

Loyalty

Professionalism

Reliability

Trustworthiness

Honesty

And you have health on your top ten. Compare health with keeping your commitments, with loyalty, with professionalism, and so on, to see which is the most important to you that should remain on your top ten. Put an X beside the one that is most important compared to the 99 others. If health is more important, health gets an X. If commitment is more important than health, commitment gets an X. That's called the forced choice technique. This doesn't mean that you eliminate all the others, you are just refining your list of what's most important down to a top ten.

After 10 days (or 5 days depending on how fast you want to work through it), the next step is to compare each of those to see if any of your top 10 conflict exists with the others. If one does, you'll need to further clarify to make sure there are no conflicts.

Before you begin, let's be clear that you are not trying to define your goals here. Goals are specific actions and targets, like buying a new car or taking a trip.

WHAT YOU ARE LOOKING FOR ARE CORE VALUES THAT WILL ADD PASSION AND VALUE TO DIRECT YOUR LIFE.

Twenty-seven

Do Not Procrastinate

"Opt out of procrastination now and make success at ANYTHING an imperative rather than an alternative."

--- Jim Britt

In times past, just as sailors used the North Star to navigate their ships, you too must use your own personal North Star—your dreams and goals—to navigate yourself to complete your daily priorities.

Following your North Star and making your dreams come alive requires you to be fearless, bold, and be self-confident. To attain wealth, you must have the determination that no outside force, or internal dialog, will prevent you from victory.

And whatever you do, do not let the mother of all resistance forces enter the picture… procrastination. Procrastination will unfailingly try to stop you from reaching your desired results. Wrap your mind around the idea that procrastination can be a guiding force that leads to your objective. Change your perception of procrastination and see it as a tool, a compass, telling you that you are off course. The bigger the goal you are attempting to reach, and the more important the goal, the more procrastination and internal resistance you will feel toward pursuing it. In addition, the closer you get to your destination the more you will experience procrastination.

When procrastination feels that you are building momentum and will soon reach your destination, it hits the panic button and starts talking trash.

"Relax, you are working too hard."

"Who are you to start a business?"

"I don't take action until everything is just perfect."

"Get it right. I have to get everything right before I begin."

"I'm afraid. I don't know if I can do it."

"This is too hard."

"People aren't responding the way I imagined."

And so on. When you get close to the finish line, procrastination will launch a psychological assault. It does everything it can do to snatch your dream away from you. It sticks obstacles in your path, maybe in the form of a new shiny object, or a mountain that seems too big to climb. It does everything it can to steel your focus, to distract you, and move you away from your commitment.

Each time procrastination rears its ugly head with a counterattack, you must fight back and strengthen your resolve to show it who's in charge. You must use your willpower to finish the race and to finish strong.

You are not alone. You are not the only one that experiences procrastination. We all have to deal with it. It will always be a part of your life. So, if it will always be a part of your life, if you don't want it to take its toll on your life and performance, you must adjust the way you perceive it. Look at it as a signal that you are off course.

Make the tough decisions now to overcome procrastination; the price will be too high later. You get paid for making tough decisions, for overcoming procrastination; that's what shapes your life, business, and your wealth. Anyone can make the easy decisions, and you will make some wrong decisions, but if you measure regularly, you can adjust quickly. Procrastination is a chronic and necessary part of decision making and the human condition. Learning how to power through is perhaps one of the greatest lessons you can learn. I assure you, if procrastination couldn't be beaten, there would be no Mount Rushmore, no airplanes, no Man on the Moon, no computers, no cell phones, etc.

So how do you do it? How do you avoid becoming another notch in procrastination's belt? How do you avoid becoming another victim or casualty of procrastination? The answer is quite simple. Your desire and determination must be stronger than the pull of procrastination. You have to own the thrill of victory. You must have a burning desire to improve your condition, the passion that drives your behavior, and the capacity to dare mighty things.

I am always reminded of a quote by Theodore Roosevelt I had printed on the back of my first business card: *"Far better it is to dare mighty things, to win glorious triumphs, than to rank with those poor spirits that neither enjoy much nor suffer much, because they live in a gray twilight that knows not victory or defeat."*

Once again, we live in a black and white world, not a gray world where most people live. Just remember, when you give in to procrastination, it is taking you away from your desired results and leading you into a gray world where reality does not exist.

Your primary responsibility is to become the superhero of your own story; the super hero that courageously takes on and overcomes every challenge, who confronts and defeats the evil counterpart known as procrastination, and who refuses to be victimized in any way, shape, or form.

Procrastination is a dream destroyer. It's like a big bomb exploding violently on the things you deeply cherish. Boom!! (loud);-)) After the explosion, all that's left are regrets. Regrets that make you sick inside. It's like an internal earthquake that leaves us feeling empty. When you procrastinate, you walk 2 steps forward, then retreat 3 steps back.

Procrastination will wipe out your bank account. Think about how much money it has cost you up to now? What could you have done with that extra money? What could you have given your family? How many people could you have helped with that extra time? How much more could you have enjoyed your life?

If you have this disease, what if you don't overcome it? Frightening huh?

How will you FEEL being in this same place 2 years from now? Not good, I'll bet!

Feel it NOW. Will you accept it? Are you ready to change? Are you ready for an awesome day, month, year? Are you ready to live life on your own terms? Are you?

What does it take? It takes concentration. Discovering how to concentrate and overcome procrastination is the key. Your progress can happen as fast as Carl Lewis ran the 100-yard dash if you focus.

Time is always ruthlessly passing us by. It waits on no one. Time doesn't procrastinate, it moves! Procrastination is the thief of time, profit, and living the life you want. Run from it. NOW. Let's do this!!

Procrastination destroys more dreams that anything else. It understands nothing but brute force. It's a world-class dream stealer. It refuses to give an inch. It never turns the other cheek, and it refuses to listen to reason.

To overcome and power your way through procrastination, there's only one way. You must confront it. You must see it for what it is, a diversion. You must fight your way through it when it rears its ugly head. You must use it as a compass, telling you that you are off course, to navigate yourself to success.

In short, you must become your own superhero, because no one else is going to show up to help you.

It takes courage and willpower to overcome procrastination. It takes character to do the right thing when the going gets tough. It takes tenacity to make your dreams come alive in the present and not some far distant future—the someday that never happens. And if you're not the superhero of your own story, then you're missing the whole point of being human.

Never forget that in this very moment, you can change your life; because this moment is all you have. It's where the action takes place. There never was a moment, and never will be, when you are without the power to alter your course. This moment, you can decide to turn the tables on procrastination. This moment, you can begin doing the work that needs to be done.

I do know this: procrastination will be an ongoing problem for you if you don't choose to become your own superhero and engage in heroic behavior that stops procrastination in its tracks.

If you want to win the game of wealth, and win big, you cannot allow the temptations and devastating effects of procrastination to control your destiny. You can no longer use the victim language or engage in cowardly behavior. Remember, behavior never lies. Do it. Power your way through procrastination and don't let it take a toll on what you are destined to create. Become your own superhero, because when you can stand on your own two feet, when you confront and overcome procrastination, you stand ready to unleash your greatness.

What does it take to win? Heart! I believe that in order to win big, it takes more heart than talent! I don't care what your current level of success is or what you've accomplished in the past. I care most about how much heart you are bringing to the table and so does the world. How bad do you want it? Are you willing to commit to your dreams? Really commit?

We were all born to be wealthy. "No, no, no." You say, "Hold on Jim. If that's true, then why aren't more people wealthy?" The answer is investment. Let me explain. Most people don't invest the time and energy needed to develop their skill sets. Most people don't invest enough in themselves to cultivate their natural strengths. Most people don't invest enough time doing the things that will earn them the right to success. Most people let procrastination run their lives.

Imagine this. You are 99 years old; one day before your 100th birthday, you're sitting on the front porch of your home. You start thinking about so many of the great things in your life, but then a regret finds its way into your mind. You get sad because you never turned something you enjoyed into an empire of profits. You rock back on your chair and let out a sigh. A tear could form, if you let it.

You think back over the last 100 years and look at all you have accomplished. Was it what you dreamed your life would be? Did you accomplish all you wanted, or did you allow procrastination to steal your dreams? What legacy are you leaving? What example did you set for others to follow? I would encourage you to take some time and pretend that you are that person sitting on the front porch contemplating what you have done with your life, what you have accomplished, and what legacy you are going to leave.

If you have never jumped on the bus called the, "Financial Freedom Express," you better do it now. It's leaving the station right now. Are you on it?

Ever since I was 23 years old, my goal was to positively inspire hundreds of thousands of people, and one day millions, to live a better life. You're important to me. I hope I've been able to bring real value and a spark into your life that will help propel you forward into the life you want and deserve. That's my goal.

Today is the sunrise of a new day. I want to just say THANK YOU for being a part of my life.

You are special and unique.

You are fearless.

You are more powerful than you know. Much more.

You were born to be GREAT. Much greater than you think.

You were born to build a masterpiece called your LIFE.

We've all had challenges, we've all made mistakes, we've all procrastinated too much, we've all had a bad year, we've all been way too scattered at times, BIG DEAL! That was then. This is now.

From this day forward, look at the time you have left and every moment you spend here on earth like a shopping spree. You shop with your time. You invest with your time. Question is, what are you buying with your time. Is it the life you want? If not, then I would say to change where you are shopping.

Your future will be bright, lively, and fun. Embrace it. Go ahead. Make this your best year EVER! You were born with a gift, wrapped and all. A unique gift. Now it's your job to find it, build it, share it, or you can enjoy the regrets on your front porch. That decision is yours, not mine. Will you sit on the bench or step up to the plate and hit one out of the park?

Batter up! Now swing!

Spend every moment wisely!

Visit Jim Britt at:

www.JimBritt.com

www.CrackingTheRichCode.com

www.TheRichCodeClub.com

www.JimBrittCoaching.com

Email or to hire Jim as a speaker: support@JimBritt.com

www.ingramcontent.com/pod-product-compliance
Lightning Source LLC
Chambersburg PA
CBHW071212210326
41597CB00016B/1776